TRIUMPH
TR4·5·6

Autofolio

TRIUMPH
TR4·5·6

MICHAEL RICHARDS

Autofolio

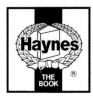

A **FOULIS** Motoring Book

First Published 1990

Published by:
Haynes Publishing Group
Sparkford, Nr Yeovil, Somerset
BA22 7JJ, England

Haynes Publications Inc.
861 Lawrence Drive, Newbury Park,
California 91320, USA

British Library Cataloguing in Publication Data
Richards, Michael
    Triumph TR4, 5 & 6 autofolio
    1. Triumph TR cars, history
    I. Title
    629.2222

    ISBN 0-85429-816-9

Library of Congress catalog card number 90-83286

Series Photographer: David Sparrow
Editor: Mansur Darlington
Book design: Camway Autographics
Printed in England by: J.H. Haynes & Co. Ltd
Typeset in 9/11pt Frontiera light roman

CONTENTS

Autofolio

It was high time that the 'Michelotti' Triumph TRs were profiled, so that their many successes could be grouped together in one book. They were attractive sports cars built at a fascinating period in the marque's history. They spanned several different periods, and seemed to do it with so much poise.

This family of Triumph sports cars witnessed the best of times, and the worst of times. It was conceived in the late 1950s, when Alick Dick's Standard-Triumph company was expanding fast, first built at a time when Leyland had taken control and was changing the company's image, then carried gamely on into the 1970s, when Triumph had become a part of British Leyland, and when MG was no longer a bitter rival.

The family was in production for 15 years, and in that time the design changed completely. Compare the original TR4 with the last of the TR6PIs, and you will see an entirely different engine, an entirely different chassis, and a substantially restyled body. Yet one change led, logically and progressively, to the next, and the family tradition was never lost completely. No other British sports car changed so completely in such a long career.

The car figures strongly in the period in which the reputation of British sports cars peaked, stagnated, then finally fell away. This was the time when British bosses became complacent, and kept traditional old designs going with facelifts for far too long. This allowed other companies (notably from Japan and Italy) to take over the initiative, and never to let it go again.

Although all the 'Michelotti' TRs were successful, their careers were perfect examples of these trends. Necessary improvements took years to arrive, and some changes for which the customers pleaded were never made. Would a thrusting Japanese company have kept the same style going for so many years? Why was a permanent coupé style never put on sale? Why was there no air conditioning option? Why was automatic transmission never made available?

In many ways, of course, the Triumph TR's 'traditional' image gradually built up because the factory could not afford to change the car. It was one thing to build 15,000 cars a year, and be proud of it, but it was quite another to use that achievement to generate the cash for new-model investments.

Even though they were always very successful, always absolutely right for the market, and always profit-makers for the factory, the TRs have tended to be neglected. When they were current models, their sporting reputation was overshadowed by other, more glamorous sports cars. Once the 'collector car' boom took off, in North America as well as in Europe, they were never as fashionable as the older 'sidescreen' TRs.

All in all, this is a fascinating story of success, of changing pedigree, and above all of survival. Along with MG's MGB, the 'Michelotti' TR was one of the very last 'traditional' British sports cars, and deserves to be properly remembered.

I hope this book will help.

The TR4's famous ancestor was the TR3A, which was built between 1957 and 1961 compared with the later TR4, it had removable sidescreens, a narrower cockpit, and a smaller luggage compartment. This was a facelifted version of the original 'sidescreen' TR, which had been on sale since 1953. All the basic mechanical features of the 'sidescreen' TR – separate chassis frame, wet-liner engine, optional overdrive and wire-spoke wheels – were continued under the new style of the TR4.

I ought to start by defining the scope of this book. Although the first Triumph TR2 was sold in 1953, and the last in 1981, this 28-year career covered three periods, and three quite different types of car.

How to describe them? The best way, I think, is to use phrases which are now well-known to TR enthusiasts all over the world. The three types can accurately be described as:

'Side-screen' TRs (built from 1953 to 1962)
'Michelotti' TRs (built from 1961 to 1976)
'British Leyland' TRs (built from 1975 to 1981)

This is the first book which has ever set out to concentrate on the 'Michelotti' TRs, which sold so well for 15 years. More and more, these days, these are recognised as an important breed of sports car, one which not only sold extremely well (and made money for the manufacturer), but one which upheld a British sports car tradition which had been founded in the 1950s.

The origins of the Triumph TR series

Way back in history (and I mean *way* back – in the late 1880s) Triumph had been set up, in Coventry, to build pedal cycles. Motorcycles followed in 1902, the

first car was launched in 1923, there was over-ambitious expansion in the mid-1930s, and the company slipped into financial receivership in 1939.

After an uneasy war-time period (when owned by Thos W.Ward Ltd), the bombed-out assets of Triumph were bought up by the Standard Motor Co. Ltd, and the marque looked forward to a new life. Henceforth, 'Triumphs' would be built alongside Standards at the Canley factory complex, just west of the centre of Coventry.

Standard's managing director was Sir John Black, a hard-driving despot who liked his own way, even if his taste in cars was sometimes questionable. It is important to realise that Standard had never built sports cars of any type.

Under Sir John's iron control, the first post-war Triumphs all used Standard running gear, but none of them was an outstanding success. The 1800/2000 Roadster was too old-fashioned to succeed, while the still-born TRX Roadster had bulbous styling and over-complex electro-hydraulic equipment.

There were several influences which then led to the birth of the first Triumph TR sports car. One was Sir John's simmering feud with William Lyons of Jaguar

(Standard used to make engines and gearboxes for SS-Jaguar, but later lost that business), another with his jealousy of MG's success in export markets, and a third was his failure to take over Morgan in 1950.

In 1952, therefore, he instructed his designers to produce a new 2.0-litre sports car prototype, which was coded 20TS. This was launched at Earls Court in October, but needed a complete chassis redesign, and some restyling, before it finally went on sale in 1953 as the TR2. The styling of the car was carried out by Standard's chief body engineer, Walter Belgrove, who had also worked with the independent Triumph company in the 1930s.

Success in motor sport, spirited performance *and* fuel economy, and remarkably low selling prices all helped the TR2 to establish its reputation. In the next eight years the TR2 was progressively developed, first into the TR3, and later into the wide-grilled TR3A.

Throughout this time the TR sports car relied on other Standard models for its running gear. The engine was a tuned-up version of the 'wet-liner' four-cylinder unit originally designed for use in the Standard Vanguard family car (and in the Ferguson tractor!), the gearbox was a four-speed 'conversion' of that already used in the Vanguard, while the rear axle was a modified Triumph Mayflower (a small family car) unit. The independent front suspension linkage was a modified version of that also used in the Mayflower.

Between 1953 and 1962, when the last car of all was built, more than 83,000 cars of the famous 'side-screen' type were produced.

Searching for a new style

In the mid-1950s Standard-Triumph's fortunes were booming, and the directors thought it was already time to produce a new style, for a new family of TRs. MG, after all, had put the smart MGA on the market, the Austin-Healey 100 project had also become a success, and in Coventry there were rumours that Rootes wanted to develop a sports car on the basis of its new-generation Minx/Rapier range.

By this time Sir John Black had been ousted from the company which he had done so much to build up, and had been succeeded by Alick Dick, who was once his personal assistant, later his deputy. Under Alick Dick a new and younger management team took shape. They all saw great expansion ahead in the United States market, and they wanted to have a new, ultra-fashionable, Triumph TR to sell as soon as possible.

There was, however, one huge problem. Walter Belgrove had always had a daggers-drawn relationship with technical director Ted Grinham, and at the end of 1955, unable to stand it any longer, he had resigned his post as chief body engineer. This effectively left Standard-Triumph without a talented styling chief.

This was the time when Standard-Triumph floundered around, not only looking for a new TR style, but a style for a new range of small family saloons, and for improvements to the Vanguard. The Vanguard Phase III had been styled by an American consultant, and history now shows us that no new *in-house* shapes came from Canley after 1953.

The Michelotti connection

In 1956 Alick Dick and his technical chief Harry Webster had one of those amazing strokes of luck which are not granted to many of us. A businessman called Raymond Flower approached Standard-Triumph concerning the supply of parts for a new project, proved that he could have smart new body styles dashed off in a matter of weeks, and eventually introduced them to a young Italian called Giovanni Michelotti.

Michelotti had studios in Turin, had close links with the Italian coachbuilder Vignale, and not only had a remarkable eye for a new line and a modern fashion, but was extremely enthusiastic and productive.

The result was that he was soon put on a retainer by Standard-Triumph, and began to churn out a succession of styling suggestions for family cars – and sports cars. The first Standard-Triumph car to benefit from his eye was the Series III Vanguard, which became the retouched 'Vignale Vanguard' in 1958, and the second project was, of course, the Herald/Vitesse family car programme.

'Zests' and 'Zooms'

Right from the start, the mercurial Italian set about producing a new style for the TR. In three years he produced a variety of shapes, but this wasn't entirely his fault, as Standard-Triumph's management kept altering its requirements; in modern parlance, they continually 'moved the goal posts'!

The original Michelotti-styled TR was a TR3-based creation, later dubbed the 'dream car', which was beautifully styled, eye-catching, and (if the truth be told) a shade flashy. The paintwork was in black and

white, the bumpers were carefully integrated to the body panels, there were prominent fins and headlamp hoods, an instrument panel positively over-stuffed with dials, and leopard skin was used for seat facings. There was a hardtop, or soft top weather protection.

Originally built by Vignale, and registered VHP 720 when it returned to the UK, this car was only ever intended to be a one-off – an ideas car – but nevertheless it had features which caused Standard-Triumph's bosses to think. You only have to look at the full-width grille to see that it inspired the shape of the 1958 TR3A's nose, while this was the first use of wind-up door windows on a TR chassis.

Michelotti's first serious attempt at producing a new TR was the first 'Zest' prototype of 1958, once again a car using the standard 7ft 4in wheelbase, 3ft 9in wheel tracks, and the running gear of the TR3A. Built in 1957/1958, this car carried the experimental chassis number of X614, was registered WDU 708, and was retained by the factory until 1962 as a

development hack. Old Triumph employees remember that it had rather a cramped cockpit, and that it handled no better than the current TR3A.

Even though it was a first attempt, there were some styling 'cues' on this car which would be carried forward to the production cars. Notable among these were the inset headlamps, partly covered by hoods pressed into the full-width bonnet panel, the scoop over the carburettors, the squared-up tail and enlarged boot space and (in side view) the crown line of the waistline. This particular car was a hardtop model, complete with a rather angular roof which had been lifted from that of a Herald coupé. The fuel tank was in the tail and the filler cap was on the tail panel, not immediately behind the cockpit as on traditional TRs.

In 1959, though, Standard-Triumph thought again, and produced a pair of larger prototypes, coded 'Zoom'. It was time to deal with the two most serious complaints about the existing cars: the twitchy roadholding, and the lack of accommodation. In a

determined attempt to give the car more stability, and the cockpit more space, the chassis was therefore modified, with wider tracks (4ft 1in at the front, 4ft 0in at the rear. At the front of the frame this was simply done by 'growing' extra side members alongside the originals, and at the rear there was no change, except to use longer axle tubes! Rack and pinion steering of Triumph Herald type (the TR3A had always used cam-and-lever) was also adopted, this having the 'Impactoscopic' safety feature, which allowed it to collapse on impact in an accident.

But there was more. This was the period in which Alick Dick considered offering a detuned version of the new Le Mans racing twin-cam engine – 'Sabrina' – in the next TR. Because the new engine was bulkier, and because the 1959 Le Mans chassis had a six inch longer wheelbase (the 'stretch' was all ahead of the cockpit, in the engine bay area), such a lengthened

Above left: In 1958 Michelotti proposed this body style for a new TR4. Coded 'Zest', it combined the TR3A's rolling chassis with a new styling theme. The removable hardtop was that of the Triumph Herald Coupé – itself still a secret development at the time. After being rendered obsolete by later 'Zest' models the factory used it as a development 'hack' until the early 1960s.
Above right: Two TR 'Zoom' prototypes were built in 1959, with different styling details on the same basic shape. This was an evolution of the original 1958 'Zest', but had a six inch longer wheelbase and wider track dimensions. Road-going versions of the 'Sabrina' twin-cam racing car engine were fitted.

frame was also chosen for the 'Zooms'.

For this bulkier chassis, Michelotti then produced a wider, smoother, and rather more bland body style for these cars, which carried the chassis numbers X644 and X645, and were registered YKV 259 and YKV 260 respectively. Both cars, at first, were fitted with twin-SU carburettor 'Sabrina' twin-cam engines.

Compared with the original 'Zest', these cars had

Below: For the 1960 Le Mans 24 Hour race, Standard-Triumph built four new TRS race cars, complete with 'Zoom' type chassis 'Sabrina' twin-cam engines and four-wheel disc brakes. The bodies were glassfibre versions of the 'Zoom' style. These cars also raced successfully at Le Mans in 1961.

11

headlamps conventionally mounted at the front corners of the car, while the petrol tank reverted to its normal (for a TR) position behind the seats, with the filler neck above it. But, in styling terms, Michelotti was 'getting there'. The screen/door/rear quarter treatment was settled, while the advanced new 'two-piece' hardtop style put in an appearance on one car. There were different under-door sill treatments on each case, while only one of them had cooling vents in the sides of the front wings.

The 'Zoom' style was adopted in almost every detail for the shape of the Le Mans cars of 1960 and 1961. These four cars, however, had glass-fibre bodies and aero-screens, and used the plain 'tuck-under' sill style. In 1960 there were no front wing vents, but these were added for the 1961 race.

By 1960 it was time for Standard-Triumph's management to make up its mind about the new car. Although the TR3A continued to sell well enough, it was plainly over the peak of popularity, and a new model was urgently needed.

Product planning, in those days, meant a feet-on-the-table discussion between Alick Dick, Harry Webster and general manager Martin Tustin. It was time to pick and choose from the styling features of 'Zest', the two 'Zooms', and from the drawings which continued to flood in from Turin.

In the meantime, Webster's engineers had discovered that there was no need for a lengthened wheelbase after all (a 'Sabrina' engine was later fitted

Test driver Roy Smith 'wading' a prototype TR4 at the MIRA proving grounds in 1961, as part of the test programme for the new car. Even though the TR4's chassis was closely related to that of the TR3A, it was still necessary to test every detail to make sure that the new body style matched the established engineering.

By the early 1960s Standard-Triumph's Canley complex almost filled a huge triangular tract of land to the west side of Coventry. This aerial shot shows the Coventry (A45) by-pass at the bottom of the frame, while Coventry's city centre is in the haze at the top of the shot. The main manufacturing and assembly lines are in the middle of the picture, the sales and engine manufacturing plant is bottom right, while the design and experimental block is bottom left. Today this site has been extensively redeveloped, and is the HQ of Rover Cars.

to a production TR4, without too much pushing and shoving).

Michelotti was therefore asked to produce the definitive 'Zest' (the 'Zoom' name was reserved for lengthened wheelbase cars), which was really an amalgam of all his proposals. Because time was so short, tooling of the new bodyshell began before the first true TR4 prototype (X664, later registered as 9123 HP), took shape early in 1961, and only two more prototypes were built before pilot production in the summer of 1961.

Does all this haste sound risky? Probably not, because much endurance running, testing, and development, had already been carried out on existing prototypes, yet there was little opportunity to check out the wort h of the new bodyshell before it began to be built, in numbers.

In any case, two other prototypes, officially called TR3Bs, but affectionately known as 'Betas', had also been built. These used wide-track TR4-style chassis, but were clothed in modified TR3A bodies, where the extra wheel tracks were accommodated under widened front and rear wings. These cars were *not* the same as the TR3Bs which went into production in 1962, which had normal-width chassis.

Standard-Triumph's development workshops were incredibly busy at this time, with the Herald 1200 just launched, the six-cylinder Vitesse project well on the way, the Spitfire sports car project 'on hold', and with work going ahead at full steam on the new 'Barb' (Triumph 2000) saloon. Other, even more secret, departments, were playing around with prototype tractors and dumper trucks. Even so, there was just enough time to test the new sports car, put it on to the Belgian pavé at MIRA, show it off to the sales division *and* to have it used at night, not always under cover of darkness, by Standard-Triumph management.

The final 'Zest' style, therefore, used the familiar 7ft 4in wheelbase and the widened tracks, the same basic centre and rear shape as that of the Zooms (and the more elaborate sill style of YKV 260), plus a widened and more finely detailed version of the 1958 'Zest' nose. Once again the headlamps had gone inboard, and once again there was a bonnet bulge, though this time it was to have a more streamlined shape than before.

Tooling for the new TR4

In the winter of 1960/1961 Standard-Triumph had commissioned a vast new assembly at Canley, which

was close to the main Coventry-Birmingham railway line, and one entire line was reserved for TR4 assembly. A few of the old TR3As were built there, but this car really belongs to the era of the 'old' assembly lines in another part of the Canley complex, which was further east.

The most important innovation of the new car was its body shell, and this was pressed, assembled, painted and partly trimmed at a newly-purchased factory at Speke, on the outskirts of Liverpool. This building was close to one also being developed by Ford (by the 1980s, of course, 'Hall Engineering' had closed, while Ford's Halewood plant had grown to an enormous size).

Originally this facility had been a metal-working business called Hall Engineering, which was much modernised and expanded by Standard-Triumph. Delivery to Canley was in batches, by specially kitted out Leyland trucks and trailers. In the meantime, chassis were supplied by Joseph Sankey of Wellington, in Shropshire.

Engines, gearboxes and axles were all machined at one or other of the Standard-Triumph factories in the Coventry area, while seats, trim and soft-tops were all manufactured in the Canley complex. Front suspension components came from Alford & Alder in Hemel Hempstead (another Standard-Triumph subsidiary). Wheels, tyres and electrical components came from specialists, but otherwise the TR4 was as much of a 'home-built' product as possible.

This was one of the original press release pictures of the TR4, as unveiled in 1961. The semi-overhead view emphasises how much wider the new car appeared to be, especially in the cockpit area. Also obvious is the smart 'power bulge' over the carburettors, and the much increased space behind the seats.

Launching the TR4

In 1960 and 1961, when Standard-Triumph was tooling up to make the TR4, the company was in considerable financial trouble. At the end of 1960 the losses were building up so rapidly that Alick Dick was forced to accept a take-over from Leyland Motors of Lancashire.

From time to time, during that winter, every new-car project at Canley, not only the TR4, was in danger of being cancelled at one time or another, but 'Zest' always avoided the chop, and the first 'off-tools' shells were ready by mid-summer 1961.

By all accounts, the transition from TR3A to TR4 was very smoothly carried out. There were two reasons for this. One was that the TR4's chassis and running gear were modified versions of the old TR3A types, and the other was that the TR4's body shell came from new facilities where there had been no need to clear out the TR3A shell in advance.

According to records now held by the British Motor Industry Heritage Trust, the first 'off-tools' TR4, carrying commission number CT1L, was built on 18 July 1961. There was a break for annual holidays at about this time, and a slow build-up (and filling of the production 'pipeline'), but by the end of calendar year 1961 more than 2,600 other cars had also been

assembled; by that time 2,470 had already been delivered, all but ten of them going overseas.

Even so, when the TR4 was launched at the beginning of September 1961, total production could be measured in dozens, rather than thousands, and many customers had to wait until the spring of 1962 for their orders to be met.

TR4 technicalities

As I have already made clear, the TR4's chassis was a modified version of that which had been used under the 'sidescreen' TRs for the previous eight years. This was a sturdy (if not entirely rigid) assembly, with box section side members, cruciform bracing across the centre (under the transmission), and with braced towers to support the independent front suspension.

Updates for the TR4 included additional members at the front to allow the front wishbone pivots to be pushed further outboard (two inches each side), and pick-up brackets for the rack and pinion steering. As before, there was a bolt-on tubular brace between the front suspension towers which could be removed to facilitate engine removal.

Front suspension was TR3A type, with coil springs and wishbones, but no anti-roll bar, while rear suspension was by stiff half-elliptic springs; the rear

The TR4 was introduced in the autumn of 1961, when it was available with a choice of 2.0 or 2.2-litre engines, with disc or wire-spoke wheels, and with soft-top, hardtop or 'Surrey' top body-styles. This was the popular hardtop derivative, and in this particular case the car has been fitted with spotlamps after delivery.

axle rode *above* the main chassis side members, which limited the bump and rebound movements quite considerably. Steering was rack and pinion while, as ever, there were lever arm dampers at the rear.

The engine was Standard's famous old 'wet-liner' four-cylinder lump. In standard form it was a 2,138 cc unit, in exactly the 100 bhp tune as that which was optional on TR3As, while the old 1,991 cc size remained as an option.

As usual, it was backed by a four-speed remote-control gearbox, with optional overdrive, but this time there was a major difference. The TR3A's box had been a four-speed conversion of the sturdy three-speeder already used in Standard Vanguards, but with an unsynchronised first gear. With an eye to future models, Standard-Triumph had embarked on a redesign. Not only would the four-speed gear cluster be made available on cars like the Vanguard Six, but a redesign, to incorporate a synchronised first gear, would be standard on the new TR4, and new cars like the Triumph 2000 (which was being planned). Compared with the old box, the new box had a different casing, and was 0.44in longer.

The TR4's chassis was based on that of the earlier TR2/3/3A models, but was wider and stiffer at the front, to support wider wheel tracks and rack and pinion steering. In addition, the new car had an all-synchromesh gearbox. Laycock overdrive was optional, but was not fitted to this particular chassis.

Front view of the complete chassis of the TR4, showing that the new rack and pinion steering was neatly incorporated ahead of the wishbone suspension, but behind the line of the radiator. The hole in the radiator block was to give startling handle access to the front of the engine – a charming anachronism. This shot emphasises the way that the SU carburettors stuck up beyond the line of the tappet cover, which necessitated the bulge in the bonnet panel.

Above left: Inlet side of the TR4's 2.2-litre 'wet-liner' engine, showing the twin SU carburettors, and the simple flame-trap air cleaners. Very few TR engine bays looked as good as this – even when they were first manufactured!

Above right: Paul Palmer's TR4 – which is registered UTR4 – has been on the concours scene for some years, and always looks pristine when inspected by the judges. There was a lot of space in the engine bay for maintenance to be carried out; this is the 'ignition side' of the reliable 'wet-liner' engine, with all the electrics and fuel supply being kept well away from the hot exhaust manifold on the other side of the block.

The new Michelotti-styled body

Michelotti's style speaks for itself, so I will not try to describe it. There were, however, several innovations which made the TR4 a real advance over the TR3A.

First, and foremost, the TR4 had a smart full-width body style, with a lot more space in the cockpit. In round figures, the cockpit was three inches longer than before (with more 'reach' between the driving seat and the steering wheel), and there was up to four inches more space at shoulder width. The boot was a lot larger than before, and there seemed to be even more working space in the engine bay.

The screen was a lot deeper than before (it would eventually be shared with the Spitfire model), there were wind-up windows in the doors, and there were face-level fresh air vents in the facia panel. Because the SU carburettors and their air cleaners were not horizontal, but cocked slightly upwards, the bonnet needed a smooth but lengthy 'power bulge' to provide clearance.

A soft top was standard, but there were two ways of achieving hardtop comfort. One was to order the complete two-piece hardtop (the roof was one section,

the glass and cast surround was the other), the other was also to order what Standard-Triumph called the 'Surrey top' option.

In 'Surrey top' form, the steel roof panel was removed, and a simple soft-top, with flexible frame, could be fixed in its place. On the other hand, the top could be left entirely open, with the rear window still in place. This was Porsche 'Targa-style' motoring, years before Porsche even thought of the idea . . .

Inside the car there was a full-width painted instrument panel, which not only had the speedometer and rev-counter ahead of the driver's eyes, but included a lockable glove box, a padded grab handle below that

When a customer ordered the 'Surrey top' feature, he was supplied with this simple frame to support the soft top which then closed the gap between the windscreen and the fixed rear window of the hardtop fitment. This option was available from the start of TR4 production in 1961.

box, and face level vents at each extremity. There was a bolt-down scuttle brace between the facia and the floor pan, surrounding the gearbox tunnel, with provision for a radio installation. The steering wheel had sprung spokes, while the hand-brake (as on the TR3A) was alongside the gearlever tunnel, between the tunnel and the driver's legs.

Identification, at the front, was by the 'TR4' shield on the bonnet, with the letters 'T R I U M P H' being picked out in chrome across the bonnet panel, and on the tail, above the number plate surround.

Press impressions, and performance

The week before the new TR4 was introduced, Leyland imposed an upheaval at Standard-Triumph. Alick Dick and six of his directors were forced to resign, and in their place Leyland appointed Stanley Markland as managing director; Donald Stokes, in charge of sales, had already joined the board several months earlier, and retained his position.

This meant that the TR4 was, at one and the same time, the last 'Standard' Triumph and the first 'Leyland' Triumph, which gave the motoring press more to talk about.

The Autocar was slightly disappointed that the chassis was still so conventional: 'With the advance specification of the Herald in mind, one might have expected sweeping chassis changes on this new model . . .' Later, in its Earls Court review, a staffman commented that: 'the TR4 now looks splendid, and the treatment of grille and headlamps has at last succeeded . . . it looks a little softer than its predecessor.'

When the car was finally tested, in January 1962, there were mixed reactions about the car's chassis: 'The steering itself is exceedingly good . . . on smooth road surfaces the car's direction at high speed is controlled by delightfully small steering wheel movements. Unfortunately no appreciable advance has been made as far as the suspension is concerned, and the ride is still decidedly harsh, with the result that the wheels tend to hop over any but the smoothest of surfaces . . .' There was more detailed comment about the car's behaviour on rougher roads, and overall this was the biggest criticism of the new car. As the testers summarised:

'Despite some shortcomings, the new Triumph TR4 is an invigorating car to drive, offering eager performance with compactness and manoeuvrability . . .'

The Motor's test comments (published several months later) were broadly similar ('the ride deteriorates quickly on second-class surfaces, and quite large and sudden vertical movements are generated . . .'). On the other hand: 'The body is practical, convenient, and roomy; and if the chassis design could be brought up to the standard of the rest, the car would undoubtedly command an even larger share of the sports car market than it does already'.

Autosport thought the new car was 'splendid', reported that it 'handles extremely well and possesses much lighter steering than was the case on previous TR models. It is much quieter . . . the gearbox is delightful to use, and the synchromesh works admirably . . .'

When Gregor Grant tested a production car in 1962, he wrote that: 'The new all-synchromesh gearbox is as efficient as any to be found on Continental cars . . . the wider track as compared to the TR3 has increased stability but . . . the suspension is still on the harsh side. However there is no question of anything but first-class roadholding, and on winding

Autofolio

Alpine passes the TR4 is a sheer delight to drive. The Girling brakes are immensely powerful . . . There was no sign of fade, nor of any peculiarities whatsoever . . . One never ceases to marvel at efficiency of the lusty four-cylinder engine, long noted for its economy of operation.'

'Taken by and large, the TR4 offers a great deal for a comparatively modest outlay. It is a most enjoyable method of transport . . . nevertheless it provides comfort far in excess of that offered on earlier TR models, without losing the characteristics that have so endeared the marque to thousands of purchasers.'

Quoted performance figures varied slightly from source to source. *The Motor* used a factory demonstrator (registered 6184 RW), which had overdrive allied to the 4.10:1 back axle ratio, and achieved an (overdrive) top speed of 109 mph, 90 mph in direct top gear, 0-60 mph in 10.9 sec, and overall fuel economy of 24.0 mpg.

That was a hard-driven car, for private owners found that they could achieve 26 – 28 mpg without too much economy-driving.

The TR4 in production – 1961 to 1965

In an ideal world, the new TR4 would have taken over smoothly, and completely, from the TR3A, which had only been selling slowly in 1961, but things did not quite work out like that.

The last TR3A of all was assembled in the summer of that year, with TR4 assembly beginning to build up immediately after that. In the meantime, Triumph's North American dealers had looked at the TR4, decided that it was too much of a leap ahead for some of their customers, and persuaded Standard-

This TR4A has not only been thoroughly restored for the 1990s, but has been treated to several 'period' extras by its proud owner. The black crackle finish wing mirrors were typical of the mid-1960s when the car was built, as was the luggage rack fitted to the boot lid. Although the owner has the hardtop and the 'Surrey' top fittings for this car, he likes to drive it in this open-top state as often as possible.

Triumph to make a further batch of old-style cars. These were the TR3Bs, produced from March to October 1962.

The first TR4 carried the Commission (Chassis) number CT1L ('L' denotes a left-hand-drive car), engine number CT58E, and was Spa White, with black trim, an occasional rear seat, leather seat facings, wire wheels and white-wall Michelin X tyres. As was usual with Triumphs of the day, it was assembled in a specialised 'prove out' department alongside the experimental workshops, to make sure that everything fitted as it should. Although this job was carried out in July 1961, the car was not released until January 1962, when it was sent to Hull docks for shipment to North America.

During its life the TR4 was modified only lightly, although the engineering department played around with several modifications and redesigns which were never actually put into production.

Even in the days of the TR3A, one car (X692) had been built with a simple type of independent rear suspension, while another (X620) had been equipped with Borg Warner automatic transmission. Then, after TR4 assembly began, X684 (registered 6206 VC) was equipped with a Vanguard/Triumph 2000 type of six-cylinder engine, a second car (X741) followed three years later, while X685 was kitted out with a twin-SU version of the 'Sabrina' twin-cam racing engine. X701 was yet another Borg Warner automatic transmission car.

(Obviously the sales division was dabbling with the idea of automatic transmission sports cars, but the idea never found favour. MG introduced an automatic transmission MGB in the 1960s, but soon wished they had not, as sales were very restricted indeed).

The major development changes were to introduce new front suspension components (and a different geometry) in 1962, redesigned seats at the end of 1962, and the use of Zenith-Stromberg carburettors instead of SUs in mid-1963.

TR4A – and a new chassis frame

Although the TR4 sold very well – 40,253 were produced between the summer of 1961 and January 1965 – it came in for a fair degree of criticism by road testers on both sides of the Atlantic. Technical director Harry Webster and his development chief John Lloyd were both avid readers of the technical press, and they soon picked up the theme of the comments. The TR4 was seen to be a smart car, and a fast car, but it had too harsh a ride, and not enough wheel movement.

There was no point, it seemed, in fiddling about with details. The old chassis had to go, and an entirely new chassis was needed, in its place. What happened next was typical of the way that Standard-Triumph could achieve so much from limited resources. The basic body shell was left alone, but a new frame was designed, and independent rear suspension was included. This eventually led to the launch of the TR4A.

The first prototype TR4A chassis frame formed the

When Standard-Triumph introduced the TR4 in 1961, it represented a complete break with its own traditions. Until the late 1950s the company had no body assembly facilities of its own, but this was rapidly changing.

To build the new Herald family cars, Standard-Triumph was not able to arrange for supplies from Fisher & Ludlow, or from Pressed Steel. To get itself out of this impasse, therefore, it bought up several independent body tooling, and body-manufacturing, concerns.

The well-loved 'side-screen' TRs had always used body shells produced by Mulliners Ltd, of Birmingham, which was only 20 miles from the assembly hall at Canley. The new Michelotti-styled TR4, however, was always pressed, welded and assembled at a factory in Speke, Liverpool, once known as Hall Engineering. Bodies were then trucked, six at a time, down the new M6 motorway to Canley.

The bodies for all successors to this car – TR4A, TR5, TR250 and TR6 – were also manufactured in Liverpool.

basis of X688, a TR4-based car completed in 1962. The second car, X722, was the first prototype which was visually and mechanically representative of the TR4A, this being built in 1963.

The new TR4A, developed between 1962 and 1964, was something of a sideline job at Coventry, for all manner of new cars were evolving at Standard-Triumph, at the time. The pretty little Triumph Spitfire was introduced at the end of 1962, the important six-cylinder Triumph 2000 saloon in 1963, the racing and rallying Spitfires were built during 1964, while the front-wheel-drive Triumph 1300 prototypes were being built, along with the smart little Triumph GT6. All this, by the way, came from a department which would not be considered large enough to develop a single new model in the more complex 1980s!

The secret of the TR4A's chassis was that it used the same basic type of independent rear suspension as the new Triumph 2000. This featured a pair of cast aluminium semi-trailing arms, with coil springs mounted ahead of the line of the drive shafts, and with transversely-positioned lever arm dampers behind that line. There was a new chassis-mounted final drive casing, also shared with the Triumph 2000, as was the design of the drive shafts.

Once again the factory had to listen very carefully to the preferences of its North American dealers. This body didn't like the idea of a more costly all-independent chassis, and asked that there should be a solid-axle alternative, using the same casing as the TR4.

Although that looked rather awkward in the metal, it worked well, and sold well. An accurate breakdown is not available, but Mike Cook (then in charge of Standard-Triumph's public relations in North America) judges that around one in three USA-market TR4As had the beam axle. This type was certainly very popular with some dealers, as it was cheaper, and allowed them to do sharper deals in competition with cars like the MGB.

There was an interesting breakdown of dealer preferences. The beam axle TR4As sold much better on the East Coast (the Washington—New York—Boston axis) than they did in sunny California. The factory-sponsored racing team (Group 44) actually chose to race beam-axle TR4As, though Mike Cook made sure this was not advertised as the official policy was to promote the new independent rear end!

There is another interesting wrinkle for collectors. Today Mike Cook thinks the beam axle is more in demand than the independent rear suspension, because it is simpler and less likely to need extensive rebuilds.

The frame itself looked utterly different from that of the TR4, for it was almost 'bell-shaped' in plan view, narrow at the front, but wider and containing a mass of new material around the rear axle and suspension mountings at the rear. There was no cruciform as such, but differently shaped stiffening members running parallel to the propeller shaft and sweeping outboard around the transmission.

Except that the engine was made slightly more powerful than before (this was due entirely to manifold and exhaust system improvements, for the cylinder head and camshaft details were not changed), there were no significant mechanical changes.

TR4A style – retouching the original

As the Americans would put it, so succinctly, there was no new 'sheet metal' for the TR4A. This meant that all the main pressings, jigs and welding fixtures of the TR4 were retained, though it was still possible to see the differences from all angles.

At the front, the TR4A had a different grille, this time with a circular badge above the chrome lettering, while there was a new combined side lamp/turn indicator lamp housing/decorative moulding on the corner of each front wing. At the rear there was a 'TR4A' badge on the right-hand side of the boot lid,

with the letters 'IRS' (Independent Rear Suspension) separately mounted on those cars which had that feature.

Inside the car the main up-dating features were the use of a wooden facia panel (though the instruments kept their TR4 positions), a revised centre console (which now surrounded the gear lever itself), and the handbrake lever had been relocated on top of the transmission tunnel between the seats.

TR4A in the marketplace

The first TR4A production car was built in January 1965, and the new model was introduced to the public in March of that year. The eight-week gap meant that Triumph was able to ship original supplies to the USA, so that deliveries could go ahead at once.

Right from the start, the motoring press decided that the TR4A was better than before, but that it

could still be improved. Opinions change over the years, of course. The four-cylinder engine which had received so much praise when new was now seen as rather old-fashioned. The pundits, and some of the customers, were already beginning to look for more power, developed more smoothly than before.

In general, the new all-independent chassis was well received. *Autocar* testers wrote that the: 'new independent rear suspension gives softer, more comfortable ride with improved roadholding . . . The greatest improvement in the TR undoubtedly comes from the new rear suspension . . . much softer and better able to cope with rough roads . . . the ride characteristics have been changed out of all recognition . . . Cornering is transformed, and there is now a steady degree of understeer, with quite a lot of body roll . . .' However: 'The engine is a willing beast, with the same qualities as an eager farm horse rather than those of a racing thoroughbred – and something of the same ruggedness about it too . . .'

Motor was slightly less complimentary, for although the testers wrote that: 'the Triumph TR4A is a much improved car which . . . goes very fast, stops very quickly, and is reasonably economical', they noted also that it is not a car that always makes friends quickly . .

The new, independent, rear suspension has improved the ride and roadholding, especially on indifferently surfaced roads, but the scuttle shake is unfortunately still evident . . .'

Small development changes, compared with the TR4, were all noted, particularly the use of a diaphragm spring clutch, and the lower-geared steering.

The TR4A, in fact, was altered very little during its two-and-a-half year life. This, as usual, was a reliable indication that the engineers were far more interested in looking at its successor than in modifying the existing car. Except that SU carburettors were sometimes found on UK-market cars in place of the Zenith-Strombergs, the late-model specification was almost the same as the original.

During its short career, a total of 28,465 TR4As were built, with nearly 14,000 being sold in 1965, but with sales gradually falling away after that. in the USA, no question, the arrival of the smart MG MGB GT model had something to do with this.

Triumph's engine problem for the 1970s

Although the Michelotti-styled TR was a success, by the mid-1960s it was already clear that the old four-

cylinder engine was obsolete. Any new derivative of the TR would need a different power unit – not a modified version of the old engine, but an entirely different design.

Let me now hark back to the post-war history of Standard-Triumph engines strategy. Immediately after the war, Sir John Black snapped up the manufacturing rights to the Ferguson tractor, and at the same time he approved the design of the Standard Vanguard family car. A new petrol engine, whose design features were inspired by the success of the 1930s-type *traction avant* Citroën was developed for use in the tractor *and* the Vanguard. Later the same engine would be used in the late-1940s Triumph 2000 Roadster and the Renown saloon, in the Standard Ensign – and in the Triumph TR sports cars.

Inevitably it grew up. When revealed in 1947 it was an 1,849 cc engine with an 80 mm cylinder bore, but by the end of the 1950s the bore of the tractor version had been pushed out to 87mm, to provide 2,187 cc. Because it had a three-bearing crankshaft, it was never the smoothest of engines, but it was always most commendably reliable. The cylinder head, in spite of much attention from factory engineers over the years, was never a very deep-breathing design – indeed the specific output of the last TR4A engine was really no better than that of the original TR2.

By the time the TR4A was being designed, the wet-liner engine could be stretched no further, and a much-changed big-bore dry-liner project was not at all satisfactory. There was no more development stretch.

In the meantime, Standard-Triumph had designed a new six-cylinder engine, this time purely for use in passenger cars. Early in the 1950s a small four-cylinder engine, the 'SC', had been designed for use in the Standard 8 and Standard 10 cars, and it was later used to power the Triumph Herald range.

Even at that stage, some thought was given to a six-cylinder version of that engine, so the machine tools and fixtures for the 'four' were all laid out with the idea of a machining a 'four plus two' engine as well.

In the late 1950s this 'six' finally took shape, first as a 2.0-litre unit for the Vanguard Six, then as a 1.6-litre unit for the Vitesse, and eventually for several other cars including the Triumph 2000 saloon, and the GT6 sports coupé.

This new engine was completely different from the old 'four'. Naturally it was longer and slimmer, but it was also lighter, with a conventional dry-liner cylinder block. Unfortunately, in its original guise, it also had a very poor cylinder head design, which breathed very badly; the 'works' motorsport department had great difficulty in improving the performance of the engines for use in rally cars, though by using twin-choke Weber carburettors, and a much-modified type of camshaft profile it was possible to produce fast, though thirsty, Triumph 2000s.

It was, however, the only alternative to the old-style four-cylinder engine which Standard-Triumph could turn to, when the next TR was being designed. Even so, a lot of work would be needed to make it meet new targets.

TR5 and TR250 – power from a clean exhaust

In the mid-1960s, not only was Standard-Triumph looking to design a smoother, faster, and more luxurious car than the TR4A, but it was also faced with a growing surge of new legislation in the USA, which was by far its most important market.

American legislators had begun to clamp down on the motor car, and was beginning to force the world's motor industry to 'clean up its act'. Along the way they were to impose a complete design somersault on their own car-makers.

Up until then, the public had encouraged Detroit to build ever-more powerful cars, for which fuel efficiency was not a factor. In future, the legislators insisted, cars could still be powerful, just as long as their exhaust was clean. This was nothing to do with the need for fuel economy – petrol was plentiful and very cheap – but to reduce atmospheric pollution.

Legend has it that glamorous Los Angeles was the first to suffer from the smog which was responsible for this turnabout, but the truth is that many crowded North American cities began to suffer badly from car-induced smoke and haze, which not only looked and tasted nasty, but was thought to be very bad for human health.

The first, very mild, restrictions came into force in the early 1960s; the TR4A, for instance, had to have a one-way closed-circuit breathing device, which fed oily fumes from the rocker cover back into the inlet manifold. Manufacturers grumbled about the cost of fitting that, but there was much more to come in the future.

The first serious exhaust pollution regulations were due to come into force in 1968, and engineers all over the world were horrified by the standards which they were asked to meet. By late-1970s standards, in fact, the 1968 laws were very mild indeed, but to those

people who had never before had to achieve cleaned-up exhaust gases it was still a daunting prospect.

The first reaction at Standard-Triumph, as elsewhere, was that the only way to meet the limits would mean that existing engines would have to be detuned considerably. This, the sales force insisted, would make the TR4A uncompetitive.

This was where Standard-Triumph's engineers were in a real dilemma. There was no doubt that that old four-cylinder engine would have to be dropped, for it could not possibly be 'cleaned up' and retuned to produce the same amount of power. On the other hand the existing 2.0-litre six-cylinder unit, as currently fitted to the Triumph 2000, was anaemic enough without being de-toxed. What was the answer?

The first six-cylinder TRs

Fortunately for all concerned, six-cylinder TRs had been running around for years, and there was no space problem under the existing bonnet. I have already mentioned the experimental TR4s which were built in the early 1960s. Now it was time to take these tests a stage further.

Even before the TR4A was put on sale, the first prototype of its successor, the 'Wasp' (this was the Standard-Triumph project code for the new car) was built in February 1965. This was X747. The second prototype, X748 (registered GKV 310D) did not follow until February 1966, with the next three cars – X753 (JDU 745E), X754 (JVC 505E) and X755 (LKV 40F) – being registered in 1967. Because of the complexity of USA exhaust pollution and crash-test regulations this was a complex development programme, for two further prototypes (X760 and X761) were also built in 1967.

When the 'Wasp' programme was started, the need for more power was planned in two ways. It was clear that there would have to be two different specifications for the cars – one for USA-market machines, the other for the 'Rest of the World' market.

In a very brave move, it was decided to enlarge the engine to guarantee enough power and torque, and to equip it with fuel injection to make sure that fuel/air mixtures could be carefully metered.

Because the cylinder bores were already as large as possible, the only way to make the six-cylinder engine bigger was by changing the crankshaft to give a longer stroke, and at the same time the block

Low slung, but still with plenty of ground clearance – all this generation of TRs had a separate chassis frame, which virtually ensured long-life possibilities.

Main picture: At this distance the road wheels of the TR5 seem to be sculptured Rostyles, but close inspection would show that they are removable plates, and that there is a conventional pressed steel wheel underneath.

In 1967 and 1968 there were two near look-alike six-cylinder TRs on sale; except, that is, in North America, there was the fuel-injected TR5, which carried this badge. North American market cars were TR250s.

Compared with the TR4A, the TR5's basic style was not changed, though there were detail changes around the nose, not least the use of new 'TR5' badges. This car has the optional centre-lock wire-spoke wheels, which have the latest safety-conscious earless knock-on spinners.

The TR5 was announced in 1967, with a 150bhp six-cylinder engine. Compared with the TR4A, which it replaced, much of the power boost was due to the use of Lucas fuel injection. The TR5 was never sold in North America, that continent having to make do with the TR250 instead. Note the dummy 'Rostyle' wheel trims on this car, and the '2500' badges on the rear flanks.

casting was modified to make this possible. One outwardly simple change, therefore, saw the capacity increase by 25 per cent, from 2.0 litres to 2.5 litres.

At the same time (and well overdue, it must be stressed) a completely new cast iron cylinder head was developed, one which had better breathing, and a more rigid construction. For the record, these were the basic dimensional differences:

1,998 cc 74.7 mm bore and 76 mm stroke
2,498 cc 74.7 mm bore and 95 mm stroke

(The modified block and the new head were suitable for all other applications, whether 2.0-litres or 2.5-litres, so the need to develop a powerful 'Wasp' benefited all other cars in Triumph's range.)

The only British fuel injection system which could be used was that manufacturered by Lucas, a development of the pioneering installation which had once been raced on Jaguar D-types, and which had been fitted on six-cylinder Maseratis since the early 1960s. It was expensive, and it was only available in limited quantities, but it worked; the only alternative would have been to patronise Bosch or Kugelfischer, and Standard-Triumph was not willing to do that.

That was the theory, at least, but in practice things did not work out like that. Faced with the possibility of making the 'Wasp' much more expensive, in the USA, than the TR4A, the sales force rebelled. Was there no other way, they asked, that the emissions regulations could be met?

Faced with such a strong challenge, the engineers tried again, and were surprised to find that a pair of carefully calibrated Zenith-Stromberg carburettors could do the job, much more simplyand at considerably less cost. Not only that, but for the 'Rest of the World' specification, the injection could deal with a more ambitious camshaft profile than before, and boost the peak power to unheard-of heights.

The engines had completely different characteristics. The USA-market 'federal' engine was smooth, civilised, but somehow not as hairy-chested as the old four-cylinder unit, and it ran out of breath well before 5,000rpm. The 'Rest of the World' engine was sporty, rorty, could sing up to 6,000rpm, and had the rather reined-in character of a thoroughbred race-horse. The power ratings made their own point:

USA spec: 104 bhp (net) at 4,500 rpm
RoW spec: 150 bhp (net) at 5,500 rpm

Although the six-cylinder engine was new to the TR series when introduced in 1967, it was already a well-established part of the Standard-Triumph scene.

In effect it was a six-cylinder version of the four-cylinder engine which had been in use since 1953, and it had first been seen in the Standard Vanguard Six of 1960. Other versions of the engine then went into the Triumph Vitesse (launched in 1962), the Triumph 2000 (1963) and the Triumph GT6 (1966).

The first six-cylinder engined TR prototype began testing in 1962, a full five years before the TR5 or the TR250 were ready for production.

When the fuel-injected TR5 was launched in 1967 it represented a real leap forward in performance. Peak power went up from 104 bhp to 150 bhp, top speed rose from 109 mph to 120 mph, while 0-60 mph acceleration was cut from 11.4 to 8.8 sec.

Not only that, but the TR5 now had the beating of the last of the Austin-Healey 3000s, and the first of the MGCs in most conditions. The 3000 Mk III had a top speed of 121 mph, and a 0-60 mph time of 9.8 secs.

Not only was the TR5 as fast as the competition from BMC, but it was also a more spacious, and better-specified, car.

This immaculately maintained TR6 shows off the roomy engine bay, where there is plenty of space to work on the long six-cylinder engine.

TR5 and TR250 – the same, but different

If the engines were going to be so very different on 'Wasp', should the cars always carry the same names? Standard-Triumph thought not. For 1967 and 1968 only, therefore, cars sold in the USA would have one name (TR250) while those sold in the rest of the world would have another (TR5PI). Although they shared the same basic chassis/body and trim layouts, their overall character, and their decoration, was different.

This time round the North American dealers accepted the idea of independent rear suspension on all cars, so the old live-axle TR concept was finally laid to rest, and this meant that the same chassis could be used for all cars. Except for the cranking forward of the cross-tube between front suspension towers to clear the longer six-cylinder engine, and other minor changes such as engine mountings, the chassis itself was almost identical to that of the TR4A. The gearbox, overdrive, and rear axle assemblies were also the same, although the RoW final drive ratio was higher, at 3.45:1.

This TR5 gleams in the autumn sunshine, not only showing off its beautifully preserved style, but what, in 1990s Great Britain, is a desirable and easily memorised registration number!

Although plans had already been laid to restyle the body shell (these improvements would eventually be made for the TR6, described later), the TR5/TR250 were only slightly different from the TR4A. Once again the same sheet metal was retained, which meant that the original Michelotti style for the TR4, first seen in 1961, was still intact, but there was enough new decoration to make the new owner proud of his purchase.

There were no longer any 'T R I U M P H' letters on the cars. Both types were given new badges at front and rear. One was to the left of centre on the front of the bonnet panel, the other was to the right of the rear numberplate. At the front these read 'TR5' on one type and 'TR250' on the other; at the rear they were either 'TR5PI', or 'TR250'.

In each case there was a '2500' badge on the rear wings, close to the tail-lamps. The sidelamp/flasher/chrome strips were retained on the

front wings, while cars with disc wheels were given dummy 'Rostyle' wheel covers, each complete with five dummy wheel nuts; wire spoke wheels, as ever, were optional.

The obvious external difference between the two cars was that TR250s were also inflicted with transverse 'speed stripes' across the bonnet, and front wings, which reached from wheel-arch to wheel-arch, cutting under the side-lamp/indicator housing in each case. Someone must have thought they were smart . . .

TR5 and TR250 cockpits and facias were the same, being lineal developments of the TR4A layout. This time round, to meet new regulations, the steering wheels had padded spokes, there were restyled knobs and switches, and instead of fresh air grilles at the edges of the facia there were adjustable 'eyeball' fresh air vents.

The first six-cylinder TR to be sold in North America was the TR250 of 1967 and 1968, a model identified by the transverse 'speed striping' across the nose and front wings, and by the special badge on the front of the bonnet panel. The TR250 had an engine fitted with Zenith-Stromberg carburettors, and was sold only in North America.

During the 1970s car design for North American sales was much affected by a rash of new safety regulations. It was to meet '5 mph' bumper laws that these large rubber overriders were fitted to 1975 and 1976 models of the TR6.

TR5 and TR250 in production

Previous experience with the TR4 and the TR4A suggested that most cars would be sold in North American specification, and this was soon confirmed. In July 1967 the last few TR4As were built, and assembly of TR250 models began at the same time, there being no gap between the two types. Assembly of the first TR5s followed a few weeks later.

By the end of 1967 more than 2,500 six-cylinder TRs had already been built, but only 25 of these were home-market TR5s, and no fewer than 2,357 were TR250s.

Although Standard-Triumph held its breath, to await reaction, there was never any real doubt that the six-cylinder engine transplant had been the right thing to do. It was true that the fuel-injected TR5PI was not quite as smooth and civilised, at town speeds, as the engineers would have liked, but because it was a dramatically faster car than before there were very few complaints about that.

much so that its top speed fell back from 100mph to no more than 90mph.

When the USA's *Road & Track* magazine got its hands on an early TR250, it was very kind about the new car. Publishing its test in December 1967, the magazine suggested that the TR had undergone a personality change, and that: '. . . this popular sports car is thereby refined and improved in almost every way . . . the engine is in a very mild state of tune and could hardly run more sweetly.' The quoted top speed was 107mph, and acceleration was almost exactly the same as that recorded for the TR4A.

Perhaps the chassis settings were a little too soft for the testers who wrote that this: '. . . results in considerably fore-and-aft bobbing at shift points, butexcept for that we found little to complain about. The steering is sharp . . .'

The summary was rather mixed:

'Offsetting the TR250's new-found powerplant smoothness and interior conveniences is a body structure well behind modern standards in terms of strength and resistance to rattles. An entirely new model would have been more exciting to us and to the customers, but the British car industry moves slowly these days, and the TR250 is a real improvement over the TR4A.'

British press reaction to the TR5, on the other hand, was much more enthusiastic, and deservedly so. Not only was the TR5 a glamorous car, with its new fuel-injected engine, but it was almost 50 per cent more powerful than its predecessor, and had much higher performance.

Motor headlined its test report: 'Invigorating injection', and commented that the car had 'Tremendous performance from fuel injection engine.' Also: '. . . this magnificent power unit is the answer to an enthusiast's prayer. Once above its rather lumpy idle it explodes its torque on to the road with effortless ease to the accompaniment of a melodious howl from the exhaust which must delight even the most decibel conscious ear.'

Autocar was equally smitten, for its summary included 'Vivid acceleration, 120mph top speed' and 'Expensive but very enjoyable'. The testers also wrote that: 'Compared with its predecessors, the TR5 is a complete transformation. As we have remarked before, the heart of a car is its engine and the TR5 has an eager unit which responds just as a sports car driver wants. The rest of the car is traditional rather than dated, well modernised, so that overall and above all it

As far as the TR250 was concerned, management was relieved that it could offer a 'de-toxed' car which was equally as fast as the previous model. That achievement, by the way, has never really been emphasised. It is only necessary to point to the way that the Triumph's deadly rival, the MGB, became progressively slower and slower in the next decade, so

is very much a fun car still.'

It is worth noting that radial ply tyres were standard on these cars for *all* markets (up until that time, they had been optional extras), and that USA-specification TR250s had 185-section radials.

Even so, the TR5/TR250 models were very short-lived – they were only actually in series production for about 14 months (August 1967 to September 1968) – and a completely restyled car, the TR6, then took over.

TR6 – a new style by Karmann

By the time the media criticised the style of the new TR5 and TR250 models, Triumph was well on the way to replacing it. In 1967, and well before the TR5/TR250 was ready to go into production, work had begun on a new model which would eventually become the TR6.

In an ideal world, no doubt, Triumph would have liked to produce a brand new car – new chassis, new running gear, and new body style – but this was not possible. Triumph, like MG, had discovered that sports cars did not sell enough for frequent restyling to be economically possible; any change, in other words, would have to be a major facelift, rather than a completely new style. Inparticular, the running gear, and the chassis, would be left alone.

However, whereas MG had revealed the MGB, then done little to improve it over the years, Triumph had already achieved a lot. In 1965 the chassis had been revised, in 1967 a new engine was installed and now – for 1969 – it was time to change the body. For 1969, and the TR6, the car would be almost

Wherever two or more TR owners get together, they tend to go off and enjoy a drive through twisty and narrow lanes. Here a TR4A leads a TR6 through wooded territory in the north-east of England.

'Michelotti' TRs were built from 1961 to 1976, and this group shows three different versions. FRO 10G is a fuel-injected TR5, SVN 64D is a TR4A, while the car in the background is a Karmann-retouched TR6 showing the final style of road wheel.

completely different from the original TR4 of 1961.

When the time came to rejuvenate the TR's body style, Triumph's natural inclination was to turn to its original stylist, Giovanni Michelotti, to do the job. This was not possible, for two major reasons.

One was that the little Italian was far too busy. At that time he was totally committed to working on a restyled 2000 saloon (which became the Mk 2 of 1969) and on the 1500/Toledo family cars which were to follow in 1970. There was also the 2+2-seater Stag, which was still at a formative stage.

The other reason, which had happened quite by coincidence, was that the West German coachbuilder Karmann (of Osnabruck), was expanding and had begun to offer its skills around the industry. One of its services, which attracted several car makers, was that it could style cars, build prototypes, construct and prove the tooling and, if necessary, build the shells in quantity as well. It could also, it claimed, do all this far faster than the manufacturers themselves. In recent years it had begun building 2000CS coupés for BMW, and word had got around.

The problem with a picture like this is that the average red-blooded male tends to get distracted . . . the car, if you can concentrate for a minute, is an early-specification TR6, complete with optional wire-spoke wheels. Helped along by the Karmann facelift, the TR6 had a larger boot than the original TR4/TR5 types.

Triumph, therefore, commissioned Karmann to tackle the TR facelift. The brief was simple, and daunting. Karmann could tackle a major front and rear facelift, but they had to leave the existing basic structure. The new car, to be called TR6, was to be styled, tooled up, and the tools ready to start cranking out hundreds of panels every week, within 14 months. In particular, the new car had to be available, in quantity, in the USA by January 1969, which meant the assembly had to begin in the autumn of 1968.

The challenge was accepted, the job was done, and everything, indeed, was ready in time. The first bodies were built, at Liverpool, in September 1968, and by the end of that calendar year no fewer than 1,468 USA-spec TR6s had been assembled at Canley, along with 51 export-market TR6PIs; home market assembly did not begin until the first few days of 1969.

For the TR6, Karmann retained the same centre section as that of the original 'Michelotti' car, which included the front bulkhead, windscreen, floor, doors, and some inner panels. Karmann produced a completely new skin ahead of the bulkhead, and a completely new tail behind the passenger compartment. The style was more angular than before, yet it sat in perfect harmony with the existing layout and panelwork.

One tends to forget that all these TRs were really quite small, as this shot of the TR6, posed against a large and ultra-modern building, confirms.

39

In 1967, it's fascinating to note, there were only four *British* engines in series production which were more powerful than that of the TR6. What an exclusive list that was: Aston-Martin's twin-cam 'six', the Bentley/Rolls-Royce vee-8, the twin-cam Jaguar XK family, and the Rolls-Royce engine of the Vanden Plas 4-litre Princess R!

TR6s looked particularly meaty with wide rim steel disc wheels fitted. By 1990s standards, of course, those rims look distinctly conventional, but they gave the TR a very aggressive stance in the early 1970s.

At the front, there was a new nose, with headlamps now out at the extremities, new inner and outer wings, and a wide bonnet from which the 'power bulge' (which was no longer necessary) had been removed. New bumpers, along with new side lamp/indicator clusters, added to the new look, though for the first model year the TR5/TR250's 'fake' Rostyle wheels were retained.

At the rear, the same squared-up look was continued, with new rear wings, boot lid, bumpers, and rear lamp clusters. The loading sill was much higher than before, but Triumph hoped that no-one would complain, and the boot itself was larger at 6.0 cu.ft. instead of 5.1 cu.ft. Triumph itself contributed the style of a new and rather angular optional hardtop; this was a one piece fitting, for the interesting 'Surrey top' option had gradually fallen out of favour with customers.

Inside the car, there were modifications and updates, some for cosmetic reasons, but others to meet new regulations. These included padded facia crash rolls, restyled seats, different switchgear and window winders, and a different steering wheel with a padded centre.

Metal badges on sheet metal (thought to encourage corrosion around their fixings) had been abandoned, so there was a new 'TR6' badge in the centre of the front grille, and 'TR6' transfers on the rear wings, immediately ahead of the tail lamp clusters.

Original TR6 – few basic mechanical changes

The familiar chassis, all-independent suspension, servo-assisted disc/drum brake installation, six-cylinder engine, and choice of transmissions was retained, though with improvements in several areas. Handling and roadholding was improved by the fitment of wider-rim wheels and a front anti-roll bar, while for certain export markets 185-15 section tyres (previously for USA-market cars only) were fitted. As before, there were two distinctly different types of 2,498 cc six-cylinder engine, but this time there were no different model names. For the USA there was the 'de-toxed' engine, complete with factory-sealed Zenith-Stromberg carburettors, pipes, valves and cut-offs, while the rest of the world enjoyed the Lucas injected 150 bhp unit, complete with rather uneven idle, and with a growing reputation for being slightly thirsty.

Fuel-injected cars were called TR6PI, while carburettor versions were *officially* called TR6 (without the 'PI'), but unofficially known as 'TR6 Carb'.

TR6 in production – an eight year career

Triumph, which had been a subsidiary of Leyland since 1961, became a constituent part of British Leyland when that unwieldy colossus was founded in 1968. Several top managers, including George Turnbull and Harry Webster, moved across to Longbridge, to run the Austin-Morris division of British Leyland, and for years it was clear that 'Triumph' was a favoured marque in the big group.

British Leyland was born in 1968, prospered until the early 1970s, then ran into financial trouble, and was finally rescued by nationalisation in 1975. It was no more than coincidence that this period also covered the principal life-span of the TR6.

Between September 1968, when TR6 assembly began, and July 1976, when the last separate-chassis TR of all was produced, no fewer than 91,850 cars were produced at Canley. This made the TR6 the most popular – certainly the most numerous – of any separate-chassis TR type ever produced, leaving the runner up (the TR3A/TR3B – 61,567 cars) trailing.

(For some years that TR6 production figure, by the way, was quoted as 94,619, but more recent research shows that a number of allocated Commission numbers were never taken up. Anyone wishing to dispute my revised figures should begin a card by card count in the records, which are held at the BMIHT!)

The last Triumph TR6PI was built in January 1975, by which time assembly of the all-new Triumph TR7 had begun. In production terms, however, there was no clash. At the end, as in the beginning, 'Michelotti TR' assembly took place at the Canley factory. Triumph TR7 manufacture and assembly, however, was originally concentrated on the vast new factory at Speke, near Liverpool.

By the time the last TR6 of all – a US-specification car – was built in July 1976, a total of more than 30,000 TR7s had already left the Speke assembly lines.

The TR6-style six-cylinder engine, though with different carburation layout, remained in production until 1977, when the last of the Triumph 2000 saloons was built.

Many Triumph enthusiasts think that Karmann's front end facelift for the TR6, was the smartest of all the separate-chassis TR derivatives. It was the first of the 'Michelotti'-based cars to get rid of the power bulge in the bonnet panel, while the location of big seven-inch headlamps at the corners made the car look even wider than it was.

At its peak – in 1971 to 1973 – nearly 300 TR6s were being built every week. Although this was not enough to keep one final-assembly line flat out at Canley, it was very good business for Triumph, and it certainly encouraged the company to press on with the development of a completely new TR – the monocoque TR7.

The production figures show that the TR6, like other popular sports cars, suffered very little in the States from the public's change of attitude following the Middle East War of 1973, the 'Energy Crisis' and the sharp rise in oil prices which resulted from it, though it was hit very hard in the rest of the world. The sharp drop in 1975 was because the all-new Triumph TR7 had been launched at the beginning of the year, even though it was not made available outside North America until 1976.

During its career the TR6's reputation, its image if not its character, gradually but definitely changed. When it was new it was generally greeted as a smoother, better equipped, and altogether more civilised type of car than the TR5/TR250; it was faster and more civilised than the MGB, as fast and a decade more modern than the old Austin-Healey 3000.

By the early to mid-1970s, however, new-generation sports cars like the Fiat X1/9 and the Lancia Monte Carlo had put in an appearance, so the TR6 began to look old-fashioned. It wasn't long before the car began to be described as 'traditional', 'hairy-chested' and 'out of date'. The ride which had been described as 'too soft' in the late 1960s had become 'too harsh' in the mid-1970s. The cockpit which had once been thought roomy, was looking distinctly narrow by the mid-1970s.

Motoring fashion, in other words, had marched on, and the TR6 could not keep up. Yet as one set of virtues – style, performance, and technical innovation – faded away, another set – traditional values, unique character, sturdy engineering – took their place. It was a process which happens to so many cars which have a long, and distinguished, career.

The biggest disappointment, though, was the fact that late-model TR6s were not as fast as the originals. On the one hand the weight of the cars had gone up, while on the other hand the power output of the fuel-injected cars had officially been reduced, while that of the carburettor-equipped cars had struggled to keep up to TR250 standards; *officially* it had done so, but some owners were not convinced.

Inset left:
Pipes, ducts and wires everywhere! This is the complex Lucas fuel injection installation of the six-cylinder TR – in this case David Lewis's famous concours-winning TR6. 150 bhp from 2.5 litres was enough to give the car a 120 mph top speed.

Inset right:
Karmann's front end style for the TR6 was beautifully detailed and integrated, with neatly linked side lamp/indicator lamps above bumper level, and an assertive 'TR6' badge in the centre of the black grille.

ATR 60K

1969 to 1976
– modifications and updates

Because there were so many slightly different series of TR6s, owners and restorers tend to describe them by their Commission (Chassis) Numbers. There were four different sequences:

CP types were PIs built before late 1972
CR types were PIs built after late 1972
CC types were carburettor-equipped types built before late 1972
CF types were carburettor-equipped types built after late 1972

Even though the original CP/CC series TR6s looked very similar indeed to the last of the CR/CF series cars, there were many detail changes, and improvements, over the years. Some were made to improve the car's looks, or its marketing appeal, while others were introduced so that the car could meet newly-enforced regulations.

To keep the story as straightforward as possible, I will list these in chronological order:

Not every TR looks as good as this today! Concours cars like David Lewis's TR6 are even smarter in the 1990s than the day on which they left the factory at Canley. The facia wood gleams – only hours of loving attention can produce a finish like that.

1969 model-year cars (CP25001 – CP26998, CC25001 – CC 32142)

These were the first TR6s, as already described, with the 'fake' Rostyle wheel covers, and original trim.

1970 and 1971 model-year cars CP50001 – CP54584, CC50001 – CC67893)

At the end of 1969 there were equipment changes which, frankly, should have been ready when the car was introduced. These included the provision of reclining seats, smarter wheels with *real* exposed wheel nuts, and wider rims, a steering wheel with satin chrome spokes instead of black, and a black surround to the windscreen. The wheels, in particular, were much smarter than before.

In mid-1971 (from gearbox numbers CD51163/CC89817), the revised gearbox ratios of the Stag model were adopted; this made very little difference to the car's performance, and was done to commonize Stag and TR6 specifications.

1972 model-year cars (CP75001 – CP77718, CC75001 – CC85737)

To meet ever-tightening USA exhaust emission regulations, it was necessary to recalibrate the engine of the TR6 Carb. While the compression ratio was actually reduced to 7.75:1, a revised camshaft, with more 'overlap' at top dead centre and more actual valve opening time, was adopted. The result wasthat nominal power was actually increased, though the difference was not noticeable.

At the same time the usable capacity of the TR6 Carb petrol tank was reduced to 10.25 galls.

1973 model-year cars (CR1 – CR2911, CF1 series began)

Changes made were thought to be sufficient for a new series of Commission numbers to be ushered in. This was the point at which there was a second minor facelift, with the cars being given a front spoiler under the front bumper, satin-finish wheel trims, different cockpit switchgear (including a column mounted dipswitch), and (Carb cars only) the inclusion of special Union Flag badge on each rear wing, with a TR6 logo let in to it.

Seats had optional headrests (standard for North America), there was fire-retardant material for trim and upholstery, while the steering wheel was reduced to 14 inches in diameter (it had originally been 15 inches).

The mid-1970s version of the TR6 in USA-market form had black bumper overriders at front and rear, and a large under-bumper front spoiler. Although this particular car spent the first 14 years of its life in sunny California, it was re-imported to the UK, for renovation, in 1989.

Autofolio

Triumph finally gave in to criticism of a difficult idle on fuel injected cars, giving the TR6PI a camshaft with reduced 'overlap' and overall opening; this reduced power from 150 bhp (net) to a recalibrated 124 bhp (DIN). Because of the difference in calibration, the true loss of peak power was probably about 15 bhp. Although the Carb engine was little changed, a new type of Zenith-Stromberg carburettor was specified.

At about the same time, the new type of Laycock overdrive (J-Type instead of A-Type) was specified; this gave a slightly higher overdrive ratio than before, and this was only applicable on top and third gears.

Other mechanical changes included smaller fuel tanks yet again (by this time, down to 9.5 gallons for Carb cars), and the dropping of the wire wheel option from mid-1973.

1974 model-year cars (Carb models only)

The 'federal' tune was changed yet again, but the resulting engine continued to the end of the run in 1976. The compression ratio came down to 7.5:1, but nominal peak power figures were not changed. From this point, the engines were equipped with exhaust gas recirculation (EGR) valve controls.

1975 model-year cars (Carb models only, ending at CF39991)

There were no official TR6PI cars in this sequence, as 1974 model-year cars were continued until the model ran out in January 1975.

To meet new crash-resistant regulations in North America, the TR6 Carb was fitted with big black bumper over-riders at front and rear. In this year only, the engines were fitted with air injection to the engine exhaust ports, further to clean up the exhaust emissions.

1976 model-year cars (Carb models only, CF50001 – CF58328)

This was the 'run-out' year, with only insignificant changes made from that of 1975.

'Works' TRs in motorsport

Triumph returned to Le Mans in 1959 with a trio of TR3S models, which were TR3A lookalikes, but had longer-wheelbase chassis frames, twin-cam 'Sabrina' engines, and glass-fibre bodies. The team was managed by Ken Richardson. All three cars were subsequently broken up.

Four of the same chassis, with wide-track 'Zoom' dimensions, but rebodied with glass-fibre equivalents of the Michelotti-styled 'Zoom' coachwork, were then built, were named TRS, and registered 926 HP, 927 HP, 928 HP and 929 HP. Three cars raced at Le Mans in 1960 and in 1961, but made no other appearances.

By modern standards the aerodynamic shape of these TRS cars was awful, and they were also used heavily reinforced chassis frames. On all occasions the 2.0-litre 'Sabrina' engines produced approximately 160 bhp, but the cars' top speed was only about 130 mph.

All three cars finished the 1960 race, the best at an average speed of 102 mph, but because of the complex regulations which referred to a minimum distance and average to be achieved by each class of car, none of them actually qualified.

For 1961 only minor changes were made – one visual modification being to add engine bay cooling vents to the front wing – but the cars fared much better. Not only did all three cars finish the race, but the best of them (driven by Keith Ballisat and Peter Bolton) finished ninth overall, averaging 98.9 mph. Not only that, but the cars also won the Team Prize, which was a very valuable award to be advertised all around the world.

These cars were later sold off in North America, but in recent years some have reappeared again, back in the UK.

Triumph's motorsport department was closed down immediately after the 1961 Le Mans race, and Ken Richardson left the company, but in 1962 a new department was opened, this time run by Graham Robson under Harry Webster's control.

In 1962 and 1963 the object was to run Triumph TR4s in rallies, though later in the 1960s the same department developed Spitfires which raced so honourably at Le Mans, and the big Triumph saloons which were so strong and suitable for loose-surface rallies.

There were four new 'works' TR4s, all powder blue, and all fitted with hardtops, overdrives, and wire-

spoke wheels. Although Richardson's department had rallied TR2s, TR3s and TR3As for several years, no records were preserved when the department closed down, and all preparation expertise had to be regained, from scratch. In any case, it was already known that Richardson's cars had never run with power-tuned engines, and that no special parts had been homologated.

Rallies, and the competition for success, had hotted up a lot since the TR3As had been used, so with the TR4s it was a rush to catch up on eight years of benign neglect. Many more loose surface events were springing up, as were handicaps which tended to favour small-engined cars.

In the first event tackled, the Tulip rally of 1962, although the cars were given light-alloy body skin panels, the cars used 2.0-litre engines and were little faster than standard – the team was beaten in its class by Rauno Aaltonen's highly-developed MGA 1600 Mk II.

In the Alpine rally which followed, the cars had 2.2-litre engines, gas-flowed heads, tubular exhaust manifolds and modified camshafts. They were much

'Kas' Kastner, then competitions manager of Standard-Triumph Inc. in North America, making final adjustments to one of the three powder blue TR4s which competed in the Canadian Shell 4000 rally of 1964. All these cars had Weber twin-choke carburettors, tubular exhaust manifolds, vacuum brake servos, light alloy body skin panels, extra cooling ducts in the front wings, air horns and many other specially developed features.

faster than before. The result was that four cars started, three cars finished, with one of them, driven by Mike Sutcliffe, not only gaining a *Coupe des Alpes* for an unpenalised run on the road sections, but also taking fourth place overall. Jean-Jacques Thuner's car lost its *coupé* on the last competitive section, when it crashed, and damaged the front suspension.

Three cars started the very rough Liège-Sofia-Liège rally of 1962, but only one car (Thuner's example) finished the event, in ninth place.

In the meantime engines had been developed with twin dual-choke Weber carburettors (these gave around 130 bhp nett, at first, and more would have been available if there had been time to play around), the result being that Thuner's car was second fastest overall, behind a Porsche 356 Carrera, until a throttle linkage breakage at a late stage.

Although the three-car team won a team prize in the RAC rally (Thuner, ninth, once again set the best individual performance), and Thuner managed to finish close behind a Porsche 356 Carrera in the Monte Carlo rally, the car was obviously best suited to tarmac rallying.

The cars were given limited-slip differentials for 1963. Vic Elford joined the team, and set a series of astonishing times in the Tulip rally of that year. In a 'scratch' event he would have taken third place, and

team-mate Roy Fidler would have taken fourth, but the handicap pushed both cars well down the lists, and the factory had to be satisfied with a team prize.

Elford, too, was fast, once again, in the Alpine rally, but it was not a good week for the TR4s, with two crashes, and one retirement.

At the end of 1963 three of the four cars were converted to left-hand-drive, shipped out to Los Angeles, re-registered, fitted with cast alloy wheels, and entered in the trans-Canadian Shell 4000 rally. On this rough, muddy and navigational event Jean-Jacques Thuner's car set many fastest times, but in the end the only reward was yet another team prize.

By this time it was clear that the day of the 'homologation special' had dawned, so no more 'works' TRs were ever prepared for use in motorsport.

In North America, in the meantime, cars prepared by 'Kas' Kastner in North America, and driven by personalities like Bob Tullius (who would later go on to build and run Jaguar XJR race cars in the USA), won race after race in the SCCA race series. Kastner had more time to devote to tuning engines than the factory did, and was claiming 150 bhp from 2.2-litres at this time.

Study the specifications of the various 'Michelotti' TRs, and you'll be sure that the cars changed considerably from model to model. Drive all the cars, in quick succession, and you'll know that is true.

But how should I judge these cars for this book? By what they set out to do when new, or how they stack up today ? One way or another, that judgement has changed over the years . . .

The TR4 is a perfect example. I drove one for hundreds of miles when it was new, and I often drove them in the 'collectors' car' 1980s. It's only fair to say that the car I admired so much in 1962 seems to have irritating failings today.

Later on, this section will compare two all-independent suspension TRs – TR4A against TR6 – but for now I must sort out my impressions of the original TR4.

TR4 v TR3A

In 1961 my first impressions of the TR4 were that it was considerably better than the TR3A which it replaced. I thought it looked better, I thought it was more practical, more versatile, more civilised, and altogether better equipped than before. There was more boot space, more stowage space, and the TR4 was much more of a long-distance 'touring' car than the TR3A had ever been.

When Standard-Triumph was planning the TR4A, it not only wanted to use a new all-independent suspension chassis layout, but it wanted to offer more performance.

In 1963 and 1964 one last attempt to improve the old 'four-banger' engine, a big-bore cylinder block was tried out, where the old wet-liner feature was discarded in favour of a conventional one-piece dry-liner layout. The same type of cylinder head was retained.

Although the 2.5-litre dry-liner engine was more muscular than the 2.2-litre, it didn't rev very well, and it wasn't as smooth, so the project was cancelled.

Back-to-back comparison between a powder-blue TR4A hardtop, and a white pre-facelift TR6 convertible dating from 1971.

It was nice not to have draughts around the side screens (the wind-up windows fitted much better, if not perfectly), I thought the 'Surrey' top was an idea of genius (so why didn't the customers take to it, I wonder?), and I thought the face-level ventilation was a huge advance over the draughty TR3A of old.

There was more elbow room in the cockpit, which was better trimmed and furnished, the steering was much nicer than before, and I liked the all-synchromesh gearbox very much indeed.

But even in 1961, that was the point where the reservations crept in. Triumph had already been producing 'sidescreen' TRs for eight years. Surely, after all that time, they could have afforded to give the car more power, to do something about the ride and roadholding, to move the handbrake lever away from its leg-rubbing position alongside the gearbox tunnel, and to make sure that the new gearchange wasn't as notchy and baulky when cold?

One problem was that the TR's performance had not improved since the mid-1950s. MG sports car performance had shot forward – TF became MGA, then MGA 1600 – while TR performance had stagnated; to enthusiasts like me, that was an irritant. The car which had excited everyone in the mid-1950s now felt rather commonplace.

In 1961 I was used to the way a TR rode, and handled, so the TR4's behaviour was familiar enough. It was only when I read what the magazine testers were writing that I began to think again about the hard ride.

I knew that the TR4 had a harder ride than the MGA, I knew that wheel movement was limited (especially at the rear), and I knew that the car tended to skip around on bumpy roads when the axle tubes hit their bump stops. Perhaps I, like the TR chassis, hadn't moved with the times; the fact that this was normal for a TR didn't mean that it was right for a *new* TR.

The TR4, in other words, was a good start for a new family, but there was surely more to come? It was from that point that I began to look forward to another TR, this time one with an advanced chassis; the TR4A was a much better car.

TR4A v TR6

It was fascinating to be able to drive the two extremes of the all-independent-suspension TR range in the same day – to compare the lusty virtues of a 2.2-litre TR4A, with the smooth-as-silk character of a 150 bhp TR6. Brian Archer's TR4A was a 1967 example – one of the last 4-cylinder TRs ever made – while John Blenkinship's TR6 was a 1970 model with the genuine 150 bhp fuel-injected six-cylinder unit which every TR6 enthusiast wants in his own car!

To jump from one car to another was to see how some things had improved, and how some things stayed the same, to see how the basic character of the cars had changed, and to see how Triumph had kept the best features throughout.

ONX 542F is one of the very last four-cylinder TRs to be sold; this TR4A was originally registered in the Midlands in the autumn of 1967, just as the six-cylinder TR5 was being launched. To 'pick' a TR4 from a TR4A, notice the chrome strips on the side of the car, with the indicator flashers at their front edge, and the slightly different grille. The TR4A, too, has a different bonnet badge.

This a perfect way to show how Karmann facelifted the original Michelotti shape in 1969. The blue TR4A is pure Michelotti, and registered in 1967, while the white TR6, a 1971 example, shows how Karmann moved the headlamps outboard, slimmed down the bumper, and generally tidied up the nose for the 1970s.

When the TR4 went on sale in 1961, its UK retail price (including Purchase Tax) was £1,095. The last of the side-screen TR3As had been priced at £1,021. Direct competitors to the TR4 were the current Austin-Healey 3000 (£1,202), the MGA 1600 Mk II (£963), and the Sunbeam Alpine SII (£1,014). The TR4, however, was a faster car than either the MG or the Sunbeam. When the monocoque MG MGB was launched, a year later, British taxation had been reduced substantially, but it was very competitively priced, £73 cheaper than the TR4.

On early model TR4s, optional extras included a hardtop (£51), overdrive (£62), centre-lock wire-spoke wheels (£36), a heater (£16), leather upholstery (£17.50), an occasional seat (£12), and Michelin X tyres (£13). Many cars had all such features, so it was easy to pay more than £1,303 to put a TR4 on the road.

The restyle, introduced at TR6 time, seemed to make a great contribution to the character change, too. Helped along by the unmistakable character of its engine, the TR4A was still a direct descendant of the TR3A, but the TR6 was a different type of car altogether.

In both cars I sat low, and looked along the

bonnet, rather than down on to it. Because this was a right-hand-drive car, though, the TR4A also had that 'power bulge' ahead of the driver's eyes, rather like a thoughtfully-provided aiming sight for a fighter pilot; on left-hand-drive cars that I have driven, I miss that.

There was a difference, too, in the driver's view. In the TR4A the original Michelotti style was still intact, which meant that there were those two obvious ridges along the crown line of the front wings; at night, the driver is also looking along the main beam of one headlamp, rather than between them.

In the TR6, the bonnet/wing joint is still in the same place, but the bonnet profile is smoother, the 'power bulge' has disappeared, and of course the headlamps are out at the corners. The windscreen aperture is the same, but somehow there is a different car out there, at the front.

But the real proof of change was going to be in the driving of the two cars. First of all, I tried to sort out the question of the handling. When the TR4A was new, every magazine tester agreed that the chassis was much better than before, that the ride was softer, and that there was a lot more grip, in all conditions. Then, between 1965 and the early 1970s, that opinion changed. It wasn't that the chassis itself changed all that much, but that other standards moved ahead.

The ride which had felt so much softer in 1965 definitely felt on the hard side in the early 1970s, so much so that the TR6 took over the mantle of the obsolete Austin-Healey 3000, becoming 'traditional', 'hairy-chested', and even 'old-fashioned'.

In 1989, for sure, I had done much motoring in flexibly sprung front-drive hot hatchbacks, but I'd also spent a lot of time in a definitely hard-character rally car. Both had wide-rim wheels and fat low-profile radial ply tyres.

The TRs slotted in between these two types, for by comparison with a hot hatch their ride was distinctly firm. On the other hand, there was no doubt that the narrow, 15 inch, rims and tyres (165 or 185-section radials) hadn't moved with the times. While both the owners generously allowed me to drive the cars as hard as I wanted, both made it *very* clear that the cars would 'lose the back end' (break away) in the wet, and that I shouldn't expect 1980s standards from a 1960s chassis.

According to the basic specification there should have been little difference between the chassis of the two cars, but in my mind there was no doubt that the TR6 felt smoother, more refined, and had an altogether 'softer' character. In both cases, the cars had delightfully accurate rack-and-pinion steering – today almost every car has a rack, often with power assistance, but I'm sure we forget just how much of an advance it was, compared with a steering box and three-piece track rod installation. If you don't believe me, I suggest you compare *any* 'Michelotti' TR with an

earlier TR sports car.

Both of them gave that slight, but definite, feeling of needing more chassis rigidity. Once again, I'm sure we have all got used to solid unit-construction shells (the TR7, of course, was a good example), but I had forgotten that a TR of this type could feel a bit loose when driven hard on back roads. Then the memories came flooding back – of how I'd hurried a TR along a minor road in New Hampshire in March, just after the

Push an independently suspended TR hard enough on greasy corners, and the tail eventually drifts out in an oversteering slide. On occasions like this, a quick lift of the throttle foot usually sorts out the problem.

The UK price of Michelotti TRs soared in the fourteen-year period that these cars were on sale. This was partly due to the general cost and wages inflation which inflicted the country in those years, but it also reflected the steady improvement in prices and specification which took place. Changes of taxation do not help to clear up the progression!

In each case the prices quoted are the 'basic' and 'total with all taxes' for the unadorned (i.e. no hardtop, no overdrive, no wire wheels) TR of the day:

The 1961 TR4 was priced at £750/£1,095.

The 1965 TR4A sold for £800/£968

The 1967 TR5PI cost £985/£1,212

The 1969 TR6PI was listed at £1,020/£1,314

The 'facelift' TR6PI of early 1973 sold for £1,347/£1,629

The last price listed for the TR6 (Spring 1975) was £2,224/£2,602

In 14 years, therefore, the price of TR motoring rose by 138 per cent!

Variations on a facia layout theme – one facia (from a TR4A) has the original-style Michelotti layout, complete with rectangular face-level vents, and with a rev-counter warning sector starting at 5,000 rpm for this four-cylinder engine; the other from a TR6 had the swivelling 'eyeball' face level vents and more 'safety conscious' knobs, handles, and switchgear.

The TR4 was the original 'Michelotti' type to go into production. All TR4s had a painted instrument panel, but later models were given a wood panel instead. The seats on this car are the second type fitted to TR4s (the first type was more obviously 'bucket' shaped). Note the holding down brackets for the windscreen (which was quite easy to remove), and the sprung-spoke steering wheel. The TR4's handbrake was in the traditional TR location – alongside the transmission tunnel where it rubbed against the driver's legs.

winter snows had gone, and when the frost heaves were still in evidence, and found the same little squeaks and rattles.

A permanent coupé roof would have helped, but not the bolt-on hardtops which both these cars could have used. In soft-top form, though, the flat chassis had to cope with all the front/rear racking, and I thought it did a good job. It meant that driving TRs like this was a challenge, but satisfying. On the TR6, in particular, there was just the hint of too much power for full use in slippery weather.

Mechanically, both these cars (the TR4A was 22 years old, don't forget) were in good heart, and there was a considerable difference in their performance. As I had often thought when the cars were new, I decided that the TR4A needed more power to match its promise, but that the TR6 was well-balanced.

Both cars had overdrives, both of which operated very smoothly on top, third and second gears, so a back-to-back performance comparison was easy to make. Visually and aurally there was a great difference, for the four-cylinder engine tended to have its own minor boom and vibration periods, while the six was as smooth as silk. On the move the TR4A had a more subdued exhaust note than that of a TR3A, but was still a deep-throated machine; the TR6 was more refined, with an engine that sang rather than rasped.

The 2.2-litre TR4A engine always made itself known, pulled like a steam turbine from low down, but began to sound thrashy above 4,500 rpm; it was with an engine like this that the seven speed transmission was so valuable. It didn't take me long to slip back into the old groove, keeping the torquey old engine bumbling along at between 3,000 and 4,000 rpm, using the column-mounted overdrive switch as often as the gearlever, and generally keeping everything as well-balanced as possible.

The 2.5-litre fuel-injected 'six', of course, looks different, sounds different, and produces its power in a different way. Whereas the four-cylinder engine is all about muscle, broad shouldered effort, and rugged character, the 'six' is much more refined, much more sophisticated and, somehow, much less fussed.

Yet I could floor the throttle from about 1,000 rpm, watch the rev-counter needle swing rapidly and smoothly round the dial, and hear, rather than feel, the engine doing its stuff. Except that there was always a slight high-pitched whine from the fuel pump in the boot, I could forget all about the Lucas fuel injection system; properly maintained and set up, it merely works, and works well.

The TR6, of course, had a lot more power than the TR4A, and even though it also had higher overall gearing, it felt much faster. Cars have their own natural pace, and whereas the TR4A seemed to want to settle at about 80 mph, the TR6 was good for an easy 90mph, or more, if the roads allowed it.

Although the gearboxes on each car came out of the same factory, and shared almost all the same components (both these cars had diaphragm spring clutches), they felt very different. Over the years some thoughtful development engineer must have worked very hard to improve the change quality.

All early TR4s and TR4As (and, for that matter, Triumph 2000 saloons) had very notchy changes, with baulky synchromesh, but by the time the TR6 came along the change had been smoothed over, almost as if it had to match the characteristics of the six-cylinder engine. The two test cars matched up to the old reputations, and it was always a pleasure to use the overdrive, so unobtrusive, and so suitable for keeping engine revs down at cruising speeds.

Brakes? On any TR of this type the brakes are so good that one never worries about them. They always worked well, and there was never any anxiety – the limits were not in the brakes themselves, but in the grip of the tyres.

The other important difference between the two cars was the way that the interior of the cars had changed, over the years. In styling terms, the update from pure 'Michelotti' to 'Karmann-Michelotti' was one reason, while the influence of safety regulations imposed on USA-market cars was another.

Although there was no basic difference in the facia/instrument panel layout, a lot had changed in detail. The stylists and the body engineers had obviously worked hard to make the revised cockpit as practical, and attractive, as possible. On the TR6, the steering wheel looked better than before, the reclining seats fitted me better, and I thought the layout of handles and fittings in the door trims was far neater. The soft-top mechanism, too, had improved and, along with the more refined engine this was a more refined car than ever.

Postscript: TR6 v TR7

Triumph enthusiasts were shocked when the new TR7 was unveiled in 1975. Shocked? Yes, I'm sure that is the right word. The TR7 was so different, so utterly different, from the dear old TR6, that it was almost impossible to relate one car to the other.

It would have been easier to accept the new car if it had been called something else, for the TR7 was not a logical progression from the TR6.

Everything about the new car was completely different. The TR6 had always been a masculine car, but the TR7 had a feminine character. The TR6 had rugged, square-aspect, styling, whereas the TR7 had a wedge-nose profile.

All the best TR6s were open-top cars, but you could only buy a TR7 as a coupé. TR6s had separate chassis and independent rear suspension, but TR7s were monocoques with solid rear axles. TR6s had smooth six-cylinder engines, and optional overdrives, but TR7s had four-cylinder engines, and no overdrive option. In USA-spec, it was no faster than the TR6 Carb, while in European-tune it was significantly slower than before.

On the other hand, the new TR7 had a more roomy, and even better-equipped cockpit than before, with much-improved seating. One sat lower than in the TR6, in more complete comfort.

Like all TR enthusiasts, I was disappointed by the specification, and particularly by the gearing, but I was very impressed by the handling. TR6 diehards didn't like to admit this, but the TR7 was better balanced than the TR6, with a longer-travel, softer, but well controlled suspension. It was possible to go much faster along twisting, undulating, roads in a TR7 than a TR6, and a long fast journey was less tiring when tackled in a TR7 than in a TR6.

Because of initial reliability problems, and because of the controversial styling, the TR7 got itself a bad name which was difficult to shake off; the enormous potential of the vee-8 engined TR8 was never realised, for it came too late to go on sale in the UK.

Even so, later cars, with the convertible style and with a five-speed gearbox were better-engineered and more capable machines than the TR6, if not as appealing in character. What a pity that the TR story had to end like that.

Triumph TR4 production figures, year by year

Year	Home	Export	CKD	Total
1961	10	2,448	12	2,470
1962	964	14,309	660	15,993
1963	796	9,142	144	10,082
1964	819	10,657	42	11,518
1965	3	244	3	250
Totals	2,592	36,800	861	40,253

Triumph TR4A production figures, year by year

Year	Home	Export	CKD	Total
1965	1,073	11,714	948	13,735
1966	1,000	8,993	1,104	11,097
1967	1,002	2,067	552	3,621
1968		12		12
Totals	3,075	22,786	2,604	28,465

Triumph TR5PI production figures, year by year

Year	Home	Export	CKD	Total
1967	25	29	96	150
1968	1,136	1,661	-	2,797
Totals	1,161	1,690	96	2,947

Triumph TR250 production figures, year by year

Year	Home	Export	CKD	Total
1967	-	2,357	-	2,357
1968	-	6,127	-	6,127
Totals	-	8,484	-	8,484

(all sales of this type were to the USA)

Triumph TR6PI and Carb. production figures, year by year

Year	Home	Export & CKD	Export-USA	Total
	(TR6PI)	(TR6PI)	(TR6 Carb)	
1968	-	51	1,468	1,519
1969	704	1,349	6,632	8,685
1970	1,308	1,093	9,702	12,103
1971	1,288	12,203*		13,491
1972	1,720	954	10,766	13,440
1973	2,002	899	11,924	14,825
1974	826	246	11,440	12,512
1975	41	38	9,113	9,192
1976	-	-	6,083	6,083
Total	7,889	83,961*	91,850	

* Statistics for 1971 only show a combined export achievement for PI and Carburettor models.

The figures quoted differ slightly from those quoted in other Triumph TR histories. The reason is that it is now clear that several chunks of Commission Numbers, in mid-run, were never taken up, and those cars were never built.

PRIDE OF POSSESSION

There is no such thing as a typical TR owner. Every one I talked to was happy to discuss their addiction to TRs, but in the end I talked to three very different characters about the cars.

Each of these cars, by the way, features in the illustrations for this book.

John Blenkinship owns a nicely maintained TR6PI, and has carried out much of the restoration work himself. John's first TR was a 150 bhp TR6, which he bought from a college lecturer where he was an apprentice: 'I didn't know anything about TRs, but once I got in, and drove it, it was love at first sight. I'd never owned that sort of a car before – my previous car was an old HA Vauxhall Viva.'

He was only 18 years old, and admits that he bought the TR6 for prestige, for posing, but eleven years later the passion has not cooled, and he admits that he has the 'TR disease', and that he will never part with the car. Girls? Well, according to John: 'They learn to come second best!'

The first car was then sold, and John then bought a yellow 125 bhp TR6: 'It was nice, but it never felt the same as the 150 bhp cars' – so that was also sold, and John then went to work at the Northern TR Centre, where there was a constant stream of TRs coming in for restoration.

'Then my current white car, another 150bhp job with a red interior, came along in 1984, and it was in a delapidated state. But when I put it on the ramp, I saw that it was mechanically sound, and I bought it for £1,100, a real bargain.'

Then the restoration of the 1970 model began, a long job occupying evenings and weekends, outside John's normal job as a fitter. This meant stripping the car down to a rolling chassis; 'I did all the work myself, except for the paintwork. For that, with durability in mind, I cheated and used a modern two-pack paint. Restoration took two years, and almost all the original running gear was refurbished so that the car was effectively original'

'It's so easy to take the body off the chassis on these TRs. It makes restoration so much easier than with a unit-body car. Even building up the body again is quite easy because the wings are bolt-on, and the construction is simple. A competent Do-it-Yourself person could certainly rebuild the body of a TR6 – I did! When I built it up again, the shell was Waxoyled, greased, and I also greased between all panel joints.

'As far as the body was concerned, the inner structure was incredibly sound, all I had to replace was a front inner wing. The skins were bad – all that was worth keeping were the bonnet and the boot lid. There are many normal rot points; sills, B-posts, wheel-arches, up inside front wings, around the headlamp cluster, anywhere that mud will stick – that's fairly normal for cars which were used in Britain'.

In recent years John has become expert in the field of wood polishing, and told me that many TRs suffered from faded facia panels over the years because water gets under the lacquer, and because strong sunlight also doesn't help:

'You can get new facias, but in this case I stripped it back to the veneer, a delicate operation (it's easy to make a mistake and scrape through it), then restored from there.'

Asked if he regretted anything that he had done, or omitted, John told me: 'There were two things I ought to have done, but couldn't afford. One was to

replace the diff, and the other was to replace the rear body panel under the boot lid. Otherwise, I tackled everything which need doing, and the car is in good condition.'

Before restoration the TR6's original mileage was well over 100,000 miles, but since then it has not been used very much, and normally never in the rain. He does not, in his own words, treat it like 'an exaggerated ornament'. Like many other owners, John has a limited mileage/agreed value insurance policy.

Advice to other owners:

'I wish I didn't have to store mine, so much of the time. They're so much better for being run, than for standing around. Just so long as you don't let them be run in the wet, then ignore them when they get back to the garage. It's a constant fight to keep the rust back on these cars.'

Parts, however, are freely available, especially in the UK, and the USA, where most of the cars have been preserved. John confirmed that most parts were available off the shelf.

David Adams, in many ways, has an entirely different attitude to his car, a 1966 TR4A:

'I was actually looking around for something for my wife, because I already had an Alvis TA21 3-litre, which was too heavy for her to handle. This was going to be her first 'toy'.

'We started by looking at a Sunbeam Alpine, but that was quite rotten underneath. Then I suggested we got a Triumph, so we went to look at various TRs. I left her with a choice between a TR4A and a TR6, and she chose this TR4A. Originally it had been on Jersey plates, and it had been there all its life.'

That was interesting, to say the least, because Jersey is a tight little island with low speed limits, and the TR4A certainly seemed to have had an easy life when David bought it.

'The man who owned it had several other cars, and seemed to bring one of them over here fairly regularly. It had 79,000 miles on the clock when I bought it.

'The inside was a bit tatty when I bought it, and the outside paintwork had started to crack (it had been repainted several times). In 1988 I had the inside tidied up, then I knew it wanted new inner and outer sills, then a friend of mine persuaded me to have a respray.

'The long and short of it was that I sent the car away for six weeks before the start of the 1988 rallies season, and got it back a year and two weeks later!

'It still counts as my wife's car, but between us we

The TR4A always felt like a comfortably roomy two-seater, but this pose, under the classic portico of a gracious old house, shows that it was a slim car too.

have done 10,000 miles in two years. We keep it in a garage two doors from home, it's taxed all the year round, and we use it a lot.'

When David bought the car it had the conventional soft-top, but with that down he found it too draughty at speeds, and had the 'Surrey' top added; now he leaves the solid rear glass and surround permanently in place, and takes off the small soft-top roof panel as often as possible:

'With the top off, on a nice day, it's a pleasure to be out in the car. But I don't even have the steel roof panel for it. The 'Surrey' top fits well, and I like to run the car open when I can.'

David admits that he doesn't do much of his own maintenance work, trusting it to a local expert instead. His interest in older cars began with a 20-year-old Jowett Javelin, then by the early 1980s work was getting him down, so he decided to get a car that he could work on himself, as a hobby. First of all he bought the Alvis TA21 – and he had never even driven a TR before he purchased the TR4A !

'The main reason for buying the TR4A was that it was sound, with a separate chassis. I thought I could do things with it, and there was the big advantage of parts being readily available.'

How much use does it get?

'Most summer we rally almost every weekend, either in the TR, or in one of my Alvises. I don't really have time to do a lot of cosseting – the TR just gets

washed and rubbed down before a rally, with a quick checkover. But it's not a concours car – to be competitive it would have to be kept in mothballs – and we have two children, and there was no way I wanted to get involved in that!

'The heavy stuff tends to get done in the autumn – not in the winter when I find it a lot too cold.

'Once I got it on the road, it was just as quick as I'd hoped, but the road noise and the wind noise was disappointing. My wife summed it up well. She said: "It's noisy, it's windy, it's beautiful, but it's mad!". It handles very well, and the engine starts first time, every time.

'It's nice and high geared, and it can keep up with modern traffic. It brakes well, and with radial-ply Michelins I like the roadholding. It has very few little squeaks and rattles, but there's a drive shaft "clunk" that I'm going to deal with shortly.'

David is quite happy with one TR, but **Charles Pettingell** (whose dark blue TR5PI is one of the cars featured in the photographs) has quite a fleet. When I talked to him, he admitted to having a 1953 'long-door' TR2 being restored, a 1956 TR3, a 1958 TR3A and the 1968 TR5 – plus two Big Healeys, and a Jaguar E-Type.

'I've always loved cars; when I started driving in 1963 my first was a Triumph Vitesse, which had an SAH kit to make it handle. It had one drawback – it was a saloon!

'My next car was a Mk 1 Sprite, which introduced me to open-air motoring, and from that day to this I've always had at least one open sports car, for fun but not for business. I've had company cars since 1970, but none ever gave me the same enjoyment.

'After the Sprite I had an MGB, then an Austin-Healey. Like a lot of people I got bored, and wanted to change my 'fun' car often. I bought my wife a Morgan as a wedding present – she didn't like it at all – then she had various MGs.

'I'd once had a new TR4, but it was in 1984 that I decided to get another TR. I bought a TR6 first, and made it into a nice usable 'Sunday' car; it was a 125 bhp example, not quite quick enough for me, and I sold it.

'I bought a TR4 as a box of bits, planning to restore it, and it was on a visit to see Geoff Mansfield at Sedgefield, that I saw a nicely-rebuilt TR3A, so I bought it. I love it, so does my wife, and nothing

would part us from it.

'One day Geoff called me, and persuaded me to buy this TR5, which Renton Kidd had rebuilt. He'd done a good job on it, and it was a great car. It was there, right away, to be driven, to be used, and to be enjoyed. I found that it would pull strongly from 1,000 rpm, the engine felt just like a sewing machine, and very powerful too.

'There is one cheat with that car – it's actually on early TR6 wheels, still with those funny Rostyle covers, so it has wider rims and more grip than standard. It holds the road like glue.

'The TR5, well it's a super car to use in modern traffic. It's fast enough, and the roadholding is a lot better than people would have you believe.

'Nowadays, I suppose, values have rocketed, and I suppose the TR5 is a very valuable car, but on a nice day I take it out for a thrash on country roads. I'm only a 'cotton-wool' owner to an extent – I like my cars to get used.

'In fact it's difficult to get general insurance on these cars – I have a limited-mileage (3,000 miles a year) cover on all my TRs, but as I have up to four on the road at once, that's not too bad is it?'

'I'm different from some people. I can understand why people own cars to go to concours with – but I can't understand people who take their cars on trailers, and spend all day underneath, polishing the exhaust system!

'My two favourite TRs are the TR3A and the TR5. The TR5 probably has the smoothest six-cylinder engine I've ever had the pleasure to drive behind. It's nicely geared, very long-legged, and very comfortable. It's a lovely driving position that I enjoy.

'On the other hand, I don't think they are as rigid as they ought to be. Certainly you suffer from not being able to get 5-star petrol. I have a bottle of a rather special additive to add to normal 4-star which does the trick. I'm convinced that unleaded fuel is bad for engines, so I don't know what we're going to do in the future. I worry about the life of Lucas fuel pumps in the future, I can tell you.'

Charles, in fact, wasn't happy with three TRs, so he also went out and bought another TR6, a Saffron yellow colour: 'Almost by accident, I seemed to be building up a collection of TRs, so I thought I'd better go for the full set!' It now carries the number U TR6 9, but that, as they say, is another story . . .

RESTORING THE TR

A study in front ends – the TR6, complete with smooth bonnet panel and wide-apart headlamps, is ahead of the original-style TR4, with bonnet bulge, hoods over the headlamps, and a full-width chrome grille.

Because Standard-Triumph no longer exists, and all expertise has been dispersed, there is no-one left for TR owners to contact when they are restoring their cars.

Fortunately there are a few dedicated enthusiasts who have built up parts, service and restoration businesses. Cox & Buckles, of course, have been the main source of new parts for well over a decade, while companies like the Northern TR Centre of Sedgefield, in the North East, have grown up around the need to rescue, maintain, and rebuild TRs of this type.

But don't rush up to Durham and expect instant service. Even though, less than ten years after starting up, this business has twelve staff, you would still be quoted two to three years for a job to be tackled or, at best, completed. Geoff Mansfield, who owns the business, sets such high standards that he will not quote an exact restoration price – just in case he uncovers more horrors as a car is stripped down!

Geoff told me how the business grew:

'It all started by accident. I wasn't trained as a motor mechanic, but I picked it all up from other people.

'Originally I had a dairy business, bought an old TR2 to rebuild as a hobby, and with the help of

friends who could weld, and spray paint, made a nice one. It just happened to be a TR, it was offered for sale, and it seemed to be a great way of filling in spare time that I had during the day.

'After doing that one, I was bitten by the bug. I'd always wanted to do a car entirely by myself. I got friends to teach me the basics, practised on old cars, and decided to do a complete restoration. I looked round for a TR, couldn't find one, but settled on an MGA coupé instead. This would be in 1976.

'We did it all ourselves – my wife Sheila became involved with the trim – and although I got it to concours condition, and it looked beautiful, I didn't like it much, because it didn't have enough performance.

'Having done the MGA, though, local people in the TR Register started asking me to restore their cars. So, next, I tackled a TR3A in 1978/1979, which became very well-known. Well, word got around, and next I was asked to do a long-door TR2, then *another* TR2, and it was in that period that we decided to give up the dairy business, buy a garage, build it up, and restore TRs as a sideline. Well, we were soon proved wrong – there was always a demand for TR restoration.

'Right from the start we went to see Peter Buckles, of Cox & Buckles, and from 1981 we were appointed an agent for his parts. We still buy a lot of parts from that company, and it's worked very well.

'In the next few years I got very interested in the bodywork side, and I really enjoyed doing metalwork. Now, I hope, we have a reputation for doing superb bodywork. In those days, incidentally, I found that replica panels really didn't fit very well – they're still not good, even today, but quality has improved over the years. We still have to a lot of handwork, lead-soldering and then surface-fitting on most panels to get them up to our standards.

'We moved to our current premises in 1984, and as you can see we've already begun to outgrow it! When we arrived, we had to put a four-post lift in, we had to install a spray booth, we had to put an air-line round the building, and a lot more.'

Geoff pointed out that although general classic car restoration businesses were springing up all round the country, there were very few TR restorers in the UK, although more and more small companies had started to sell parts, and service expertise. Although Cox and Buckles were able to supply most parts, the Northern TR Centre eventually began to make its own trim parts, and took on a full-time trimmer.

Geoff also admits that the bodies of British and European TRs take a terrible beating from salt-strewn roads, which explains why several left-hand-drive cars were in his workshops when I paid him a call:

'American, particularly Californian, cars, have been very good value in recent years, because they don't have the same sort of corrosion. The difference is very marked. A lot of people can tackle a Do-It-Yourself rebuild on a Californian/West Coast car, simply because of the lack of rust. Getting the body of the chassis is very easy, and because this is usually sound any replacement panels can be fitted without too much trouble.'

Geoff also confirmed that it is quite straightforward to convert a car from left-hand-drive to right-hand-drive, and to turn a carburetted engine into a fuel-injected unit.

'By our standards the conversion is very straightforward, especially if the body shell has been removed for other work to be done. It's just a case of cutting holes in the bulkhead for the steering column to go through, modifying the pedals, changing the steering rack, then welding up holes and altering the dash framework.'

The parts supply situation is good, in fact improving all the time, though from time to time there are temporary shortages. In the UK, not only Cox & Buckles but several small concerns have had

components remanufactured. On TR6s only, certain panels are still available from Unipart, but no mechanical items are available from factory sources. There should be no shortage that keeps such a TR permanently off the road.

'Years ago there used to be a problem with Lucas fuel injection,' Geoff told me, 'when Lucas had stopped working on them, but the specialists had not developed. Now there are two rebuilding companies in the UK.

'We rebuild engines, gearboxes, overdrives and back axles ourselves, as do other specialists. We can get all the parts we need, and some of them are remarkably cheap.

'Wire wheels, well, supplies are plentiful, but now that they are made in India, the quality isn't as good as it used to be. We find that there are more problems over run-out, and getting the balance right.'

SPECIFICATIONS

Note : These specification details take into account variations made, from time to time, for particular markets.

Triumph TR4 – produced 1961 to 1965

Engine: 4-cyl, 86x92 mm, 2,138cc, CR 9.0:1, 2 SU HS6 carburettors at first, later 2 Zenith-Stromberg 175CD carburettors. 100bhp (net) at 4,600 rpm. Maximum torque 127 lb. ft. at 3,350 rpm. Optional 7.0:1 compression ratio, certain markets.

Optional engine, to special order: 83x92 mm, 1,991 cc, CR 9.0:1. 100bhp (gross) at 4,800 rpm. Maximum torque 117 lb. ft. (gross) at 3,000 rpm.

Transmission: Rear axle ratio 3.7:1. Coil spring clutch. All-synchromesh gearbox; overall gear ratios 3.7, 4.90, 7.44, 11.61, reverse 11.93:1. Optional overdrive, with 4.1:1 rear axle ratio, 3.36:1. 20.0 mph/1,000 rpm in top gear without overdrive; with overdrive fitted, 18.05 mph/1,000 rpm in direct top gear, 22.2 mph/1,000 rpm in overdrive top gear.

Suspension and brakes: Independent front suspension, coil springs, wishbones and telescopic dampers; live (beam) rear axle, half-elliptic rear springs, lever-arm dampers. Rack and pinion steering. 10.9 in diameter front disc brakes, 9x1.75 in. rear drum brakes. Various section cross-ply or radial-ply tyres. Disc or centre-lock wire spoke wheels, 4.0 in rim width.

Dimensions: Wheelbase 7 ft 4 in (223.5 cm); front track 4 ft 1 in (124.5 cm); rear track 4 ft 0 in (122 cm): overall length 12 ft 10 in (391 cm); width 4 ft 9.5 in (146 cm); height (soft-top erect) 4 ft 2 in (127 cm). Turning circle 33 ft 0 in (10.1 m). Fuel tank 11.75 Imp gal (53.5 l). Unladen weight 2,240 lb (1,015 kg).

Triumph TR4A – produced 1965 to 1967

Specification basically as for final-model TR4, except for:

Engine: 2,138 cc engine: 104 bhp (net) at 4,700 rpm. Maximum torque 132 lb ft at 3,000 rpm. 2-litre engine available 'to special order', but none thought to have been made.

Transmission: Diaphragm spring clutch.

Suspension: Independent rear suspension, coil springs, semi-trailing arms, lever-arm dampers. For the USA market only, the live-axle option was retained.

Dimensions: Rear track 4 ft 0.5 in (123 cm) with independent rear suspension; width 4 ft 10 in (147 cm). Unladen weight 2,212 lb (1,005 kg).

Triumph TR5PI – produced 1967 and 1968

Engine: 6-cyl, 74.7x95 mm, 2,498 cc, CR 9.5:1, Lucas fuel injection. 150 bhp (net) at 5,000 rpm. Maximum torque 164 lb ft at 3,500 rpm.

Transmission: Rear axle ratio 3.45:1. Diaphragm spring clutch. All synchromesh gearbox; overall gear ratios 3.45, 4.59, 6.94, 10.83, reverse 11.11:1. Optional overdrive, 2.83:1. 21.2 mph/1,000 rpm in direct top gear, 25.9 mph/1,000 rpm in overdrive top gear.

Suspension and brakes: Independent front suspension, coil springs, wishbones and telescopic dampers; independent rear suspension, coil springs, semi-trailing arms, lever-arm dampers. Rack and pinion steering. 10.9 in diameter front disc brakes, 9x1.75 in. rear drum brakes. 165-15 in. radial-ply tyres. Disc or centre-lock wire spoke wheels, 4.5 in rim width.

Dimensions: Wheelbase 7 ft 4 in (223.5 cm); front track 4 ft 1.25 in (125 cm); rear track 4 ft 0.75 in (124 cm): overall length 12 ft 10 in (391 cm); width 4 ft 9.5 in (146 cm); height (soft-top erect) 4 ft 2 in (127 cm). Turning circle 33 ft 0 in (10.1 m). Fuel tank 11.25 Imp gal (51.0 l). Unladen weight 2,268 lb (1,034 kg).

Triumph TR250 – produced 1967 and 1968

Specification basically as for TR5PI, except for:

Engine: CR 8.5:1. 2 Zenith-Stromberg 175CD2SE carburettors. 104 bhp (net) at 4,500 rpm. Maximum torque 143 lb ft at 3,000 rpm.

Transmission: Rear axle ratio 3.7:1. Overall gear ratios (3.03, if overdrive fitted), 3.70, 4.9, 7.44, 11.61, reverse 11.93:1. 20.75 mph/1,000 rpm in direct top gear, 25.3 mph/1,000 rpm in overdrive.

Suspension: 185-15 in. radial ply tyres.

Triumph TR6PI – produced 1968 to 1975

Engine: 6-cyl, 74.7x95 mm, 2,498 cc, CR 9.5:1, Lucas fuel injection. (Before 1973 model year, CP Commission Number series) 150 bhp (net) at 5,000 rpm. Maximum torque 164 lb ft at 3,500 rpm. (From start of 1973 model year, CR Commission Number series) 124 bhp (DIN) at 5,000 rpm. Maximum torque 143 lb ft at 3,500 rpm.

Transmission: Rear axle ratio 3.45:1. Diaphragm spring clutch. All synchromesh gearbox; original cars had overall gear ratios 3.45, 4.59, 6.94, 10.83, reverse

11.11:1. Optional overdrive, 2.83:1.
21.2 mph/1,000 rpm in direct top gear;
25.9 mph/1,000 rpm in overdrive top gear.

From Gearbox Numbers CD51163/CC89817 (in mid-1971), revised gear ratios were 3.45, 4,78, 7.25, 10.33, reverse 11.62:1.

From early 1973 model year, Commission Numbers CR567, the J-Type overdrive option replaced the original A-Type overdrive option. The new overall overdrive ratio was 2.75:1, 26.6 mph/1,000 rpm in overdrive top gear.

Suspension and brakes: Independent front suspension, coil springs, wishbones, anti-roll bar and telescopic dampers; independent rear suspension, coil springs, semi-trailing arms, lever-arm dampers. Rack and pinion steering. 10.9 in diameter front disc brakes, 9x1.75 in. rear drum brakes. 165-15 or 185-15 radial-ply tyres. Disc or centre-lock wire spoke wheels, 5.0 in. (some 5.5 in.) rim width.

Dimensions: Wheelbase 7 ft 4 in (223.5 cm); front track 4 ft 2.25 in (127.5 cm); rear track 4 ft 0.75 in (124 cm): overall length 13 ft 3 in (404 cm); width 4 ft 10 in (147 cm); height (soft-top erect) 4 ft 2 in (127 cm). Turning circle 33 ft 0 in (10.1 m), 34 ft 0 in (10.4 m) after 1971. Fuel tank (1968-1972) 11.25 Imp gal (51.0 l); (1973-1975) 10.75 Imp gal (48.6 l). Unladen weight 2,408 lb (1,085 kg).

Triumph TR6 (Carb – USA specification) – produced 1968 to 1976

Specification basically as for TR6PI, except for :
Engine: (1969-1971) CR 8.5:1, 2 Zenith-Stromberg 175CD2SE carburettors. 104 bhp (net) at 4,500 rpm. Maximum torque 143 lb ft at 3,000 rpm.
(1972) CR 7.75:1, 2 Zenith-Stromberg 175CD2SE carburettors. 106 bhp (net) at 4,900 rpm. Maximum torque 133 lb ft at 3,000 rpm.
(1973) CR 7.75:1, 2 Zenith-Stromberg 175CD2SEV carburettors. 106 bhp (net) at 4,900 rpm. Maximum torque 133 lb ft at 3,000 rpm.
(1974-1976) CR 7.5:1, 2 Zenith-Stromberg 175CD2SEV carburettors. 106 bhp (net) at 4,900 rpm. Maximum torque 133 lb ft at 3,000 rpm.
Transmission: Rear axle ratio 3.70:1. Original cars had overall gear ratios 3.70, 4.9, 7.44, 11.61, reverse 11.93:1. Optional overdrive, 3.03:1.
20.75 mph/1,000 rpm in direct top gear;
25.3 mph/1,000 rpm in overdrive top gear.

From Gearbox Numbers CD51163/CC89817 (mid-1971), revised gear ratios were 3.70, 5.13, 7.77,

11.08, reverse 12.47:1.

From the beginning of 1973 model year, Commission Number CF1 onwards, the J-Type overdrive option replaced the original A-Type overdrive option. The new overall overdrive ratio was 2.95:1, 26.1 mph/1,000 rpm in overdrive top gear.
Suspension: 185-15 in. radial-ply tyres only.
Dimensions: Overall length (1973-1974) 13 ft 6.1 in (412 cm), (1975-1976) 13 ft 7.6 in (415.5 cm). Fuel tank (1972 only) 10.25 Imp gal (46.5 l), (1973-1976) 9.5 Imp gal (43.0 l). Unladen weight (1968-1969) 2,268 lb (1,034 kg); (1970) 2,464 lb (1,118 kg); (1971-1974) 2,408 lb (1,085 kg); (1975-1976) 2,442 lb (1,106 kg).

ACKNOWLEDGEMENTS

Where on earth do I start – and stop – with acknowledgements? A lot of the research for this book goes back many years and many interviews, with personalities like Lord Stokes, Alick Dick, Harry Webster, John Lloyd, Anders Clausager, Graham Robson, Richard Langworth, 'Kas' Kastner, Mike Cook, and others.

This time round, however, I could not possibly have finished the job without a lot of help from:

Anders Clausager of the British Motor Industry Heritage Trust, of Studley, England
Geoff and Sheila Mansfield of the Northern TR Centre, in Sedgefield, England, for help with cars, locations, and restoration advice
Mike Cook and Steve Rossi, both long-time Triumph experts from the USA, for their memories
Bill Piggott of the Triumph TR Register
David Adams, Brian Archer, John Blenkinship and Charles Pettingell, for lending cars for photography, and for talking so freely about them
Graham Robson, for help with photography
Richard Langworth, for USA-based research
Renton Kidd and Kevin Earl, for their boundless enthusiasm

To photograph the first and the last of the 'Michelotti' TRs – a TR4 and a TR6 – we persuaded Paul Palmer and David Lewis to take their immaculate concours cars to Milton Keynes, where the new town's modern architecture contrasted strongly with the lines of the classic TRs.

Heidi Mitchell of the Milton Keynes Development Corporation not only acted as a 'finder' of the most interesting backdrops, but was also persuaded to act as one of the models.

The other TRs were photographed in a wide-ranging visit to the north-east of England. Not only did Geoff and Shelia Mansfield of the Northern TR Centre in Sedgefield beg or borrow all the cars we needed, but they also helped recommend locations.

The open-country scenes were shot in and around Hamsterley Forest, and in the village of Hamsterley itself. For a 'stately-home' backdrop we were fortunate to be allowed to visit Wynyard Hall, just north of the Teesside complex, while the balance of the shots were taken in the old industrial town of Hartlepool.

On two chilly autumn days the cars' owners were generosity itself, but the two models, Lynn Contren and Beverley Earl, must have courted pneumonia to decorate the scenes so well and brighten up two very dull days in County Durham.

On the technical side, the cameras used were a Hasselblad SWC, 500C with 50, 80 and 150mm lenses, and two Leica R4s with a range of Leica lenses from 16 to 560mm.

Colour film used was exclusively Kodachrome 25, 64 and 200 ASA including the 120 material. Black and white film was also Kodak, being T-MAX 100 (TMX), 400 (TMY) and the wonderful 3200 (TMZ), which did sterling work in a very wet Hamsterley Forest!

Michael Richards